Flash!
Bang!
Pop!
Fizz!

Exciting Science for Curious Minds

Janet Parks Chahrour

Illustrated by
Ann Humphrey Williams

BARRON'S

Dedication

To my parents, Lois and Russ Parks,
who told me I could write.
To my students, who teach *me* every day.

All inquiries should be addressed to:
Barron's Educational Series, Inc.
250 Wireless Boulevard
Hauppauge, New York 11788
http://www.barronseduc.com

Library of Congress Catalog Card No.: 99-45295

International Standard Book No.: 0-7641-1142-6

**Library of Congress Cataloging-in-Publication
Data**
Chahrour, Janet
        Flash! Bang! Pop! Fizz! : exciting science for
curious minds / by Janet Chahrour ; illustrated by Ann
Humphrey Williams.
        p. cm.
        Includes index.
        Summary: Presents the procedures and concepts
involved in twenty-five physical science experiments that
can be done at home with readily available materials,
exploring gases, density, fluid dynamics, gravity, and
motion.
        ISBN 0-7641-1142-6
        1. Physical sciences—Experiments—Juvenile
literature. 2. Science projects—Juvenile literature.
[1. Physical sciences—Experiments. 2. Experiments.
3. Science projects.] I. Williams, Ann Humphrey, ill. III. Title.
Q164.C415 2000
530'.078—dc21
                                                    99-45295

PRINTED IN HONG KONG
9 8 7 6 5 4 3 2

Acknowledgments

My activity ideas and approaches have been woven together with
strands from a variety of sources. I am grateful to many dynamic
teachers and writers who have shared their expertise through
courses, workshops, journals, and books. Some notable teachers
are:

Bob Becker, chemistry teacher at Kirkwood High School,
Kirkwood, Missouri, workshop presenter, inventor, and author of
Twenty Demonstrations Guaranteed to Knock Your Socks Off!
Volume I and II (Flinn Scientific, 1994, 1997).

Tik L. Liem, former adjunct professor of science education at
San Diego State University, workshop presenter, entrepreneur,
and author of *Invitations to Science Inquiry* (Science Inquiry
Enterprises, 1981). Dr. Liem died in 1993.

Alan J. McCormack, professor of science education at San
Diego State University, magician, workshop presenter, and author
of *Inventor's Workshop* (David S. Lake Publishers, 1981) and
Magic and Showmanship for Teachers (Idea Factory, 1990).

Terrence P. Toepker, professor of physics and science
education consultant at Xavier University, Cincinnati, Ohio, author
of journal articles and workshop presenter.

Andy Sae, professor of chemistry at Eastern New Mexico
University, workshop presenter and author of *Chemical Magic in
the Grocery Store* (Kendall/Hunt Publishing, 1996).

Other notable resources are:
The Book of Positive Quotations, compiled by John Cook, Fairview
Press, 1997.

Cookwise; The Hows and Whys of Successful Cooking, by Shirley
O. Corriher, William Morrow and Company, Inc., 1997.

Discovering Density and Bubble-ology, Great Explorations in Math
and Science (Gems) Program, Lawrence Hall of Science,
University of California, Berkeley, CA, 1986.

The Exploratorium Web Site. The Museum of Science, Art, and
Human Perception. Available at http://www.exploratorium.edu

Fun With Chemistry, Institute for Chemical Education, University
of Wisconsin—Madison, 1991.

Hands-On Physics Activities with Real-Life Applications, by James
Cunningham and Norman Herr, The Center for Applied Research
in Education, 1994.

How Things Work; The Physics of Everyday Life, by Louis
A. Bloomfield, John Wiley & Sons Inc., 1997.

Science Experiments You Can Eat, by Vicki Cobb, Scholastic Inc.,
1972.

Teaching Science with Toys, by Jerry L. Sarquis, A. Mickey
Sarquis, and John P. Williams, Terrific Science Press, Miami
University—Middletown, 1994.

Many thanks go to Paula Williams Butler, Ryan Chahrour, John
Kachuba, Julia Cross Knispel, Lois Parks, Russell Parks, and Terry
Toepker for their helpful reviews of the manuscript. I am
especially grateful to my sons, Ryan and Andrew, for our time
investigating neat science stuff together, and to my husband,
Chaker, for his loving support.

Contents

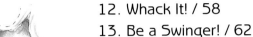

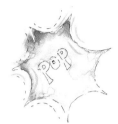

ACTIVITIES AND RECORD SHEETS / 7

Air and Other Gases

Density

Go with the Flow: Fluid Dynamics

Gravity and Motion

Structures

Create Your Own

VOCABULARY AND CONCEPT EXPLANATIONS / 119

How To Use This Book

Most activities in this book have three parts: instructions for doing the activity; an inviting space for records, including sketches and questions; and concept explanations, including definitions of key terms. The instructions and record sheets are found together in the front of the book and the explanations and vocabulary are in the back of the book.

DOING is what the book is all about. It is the most crucial step toward understanding and the most fun. Look through the Table of Contents and the instruction pages to find activities that grab your interest. Look at the materials lists and see if you have what you need to carry them out. Make your own list of any items you need to purchase. Talk to your parents about getting the things on your list and agree on where and when you will do the activities. The kitchen is the likely place for many of the activities because there you can wipe spills easily. Clean-up is the investigator's own responsibility!

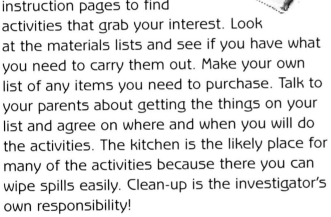

Take your time as you dig into a project. The estimated time for most activities is 30 to 60 minutes, but if you are a curious and inventive person you might try variations of an activity that fill several exciting hours. So much the better!

Although you don't need any experience to get started with these activities, it will help to understand the following three terms:

Observe (make an observation): Use your senses. What do you feel, hear, see, taste, or smell? Example: "Bubbles are forming." (By the way, don't taste or smell unknown chemicals as some are poisonous.)

Hypothesize (make a hypothesis): Guess how something works based on what you already know. Example: "A chemical reaction is happening."

Predict (make a prediction): Guess what is going to happen based on what you already know. Example: "The bubbles will stop forming when all the baking soda is gone." Predictions and hypotheses are closely related. You make a *prediction* based on your *hypothesis*.

As you investigate, make drawings and notes of what you observe and write down your questions. It is often the careful observer, the one who notices things others don't, who finds creative solutions to problems. Feed your brain with questions and see what you can discover. Be sure to admit to yourself when you don't "get" something. When that happens, tell yourself, "This does not make sense to me *yet*," which is much better than, "This makes no sense!" It shows you are open to learning something new. The concept section for the activity will clear up much of what confuses you. Still, learning new things always leads to more questions, some of which NO ONE has ever answered.

Surprise is part of the excitement of a great activity. So, where possible *and* safe, the instructions will not tell all that will happen. Try to figure out the mysteries yourself, then when you are ready, check the science concept explanations in the back. Should you be tempted to skip those sections, think twice. You may get a "buzz" from an awesome activity, but unless you understand the concepts behind it, you haven't really gotten very far. Realize that some of the ideas you have now about how things work are incorrect. Everyone carries some

misconceptions. You might as well figure out what misunderstandings you have and begin correcting them.

Do read "Thinking Like a Scientist." Science, often thought of as a field of knowledge, is also a method of collecting and evaluating information. Developing the skill of thinking like a scientist will enhance your life. It need not replace your ability to think like an artist or a poet or an athlete. Every skill and outlook you learn makes you more capable and more interesting.

If you want to learn more about a certain science concept, the "Physical Science Concept Index" on page 157 will help you find the right activities. The "Graphing Appendix" on page 160 will help you create useful graphs. And how each activity relates to the National Science Education Standards is shown in the "National Science Education Standards Matrix" on page 158.

Enjoy your adventures with these activities. Take some risks by trying variations. And share some of your discoveries, ideas, and/or jokes with the author at her website: http://www.countryday.net/science8/

Thinking Like a Scientist

Science is a way of collecting information about the world and universe. To be sure that the information collected is reliable, certain rules must be followed. Scientists, while they are each unique human beings, have one trait in common. They all share great respect for the importance of these rules. The rules become a way of thinking.

The world has never actually agreed on one list of these rules, but if it had, the list would go something like this:

The Rules

1. Human impressions, perceptions, and memory are often mistaken. So,
   a. Find ways to measure time, distance, force, and so on with good tools.
   b. Write down measurements right away.
   c. Realize that observations are different than conclusions.
   d. Keep an open mind until lots of data are collected.

2. Humans have imperfect judgment. They are biased, think wishfully, and some are dishonest. Even written data can be misleading. So,
   a. Clearly state questions to be answered.
   b. Design experiments that are clever enough to prevent bias and dishonesty from affecting the results.
   c. Design experiments so that only one factor (such as weight, temperature, or color) is investigated at a time.
   d. In the experiments, carefully keep each factor, except for the tested factor, the same for each try.

3. Sources of error will still creep in. So,
   a. Do many trials with the same conditions so that imperfections that occur will tend to average out.
   b. Be sure others repeat your results before you trust them too much. Maybe there was an error you could not see.
   c. Be open to the idea that new information may, in the future, show new truths not clear now.

These rules do not come naturally to most people. Practice is needed to know how to apply them. There is another side, though, to thinking like a scientist, a side that you were born with. It is open curiosity and a great imagination. Good scientists are delighted by the workings of the natural world.

If you are curious about why rockets fly, what makes ice cream creamy, or why the shower curtain likes to stick to you, you have what it takes to enjoy this book and practice some aspects of *Thinking Like a Scientist*.

A Note to Parents

May this book guide your child through hours of delight in exploring the natural world. If you are lucky enough to be invited to join in on some of the activities with your child, be sure to model curiosity and a sense of wonder. Answer questions, but, to preserve precious investigative zeal, don't be too helpful, or too full of information. Instead, reinforce your child's abilities and pose "why?" and "what if?" questions. Enjoy the time you spend doing investigations with your child. It will promote love of learning and positive self-esteem for both of you!

Excitement and danger tend to go hand-in-hand. Therefore, some of the activities in this book have warnings. The candle and stove top heat sources used in "Implosion!" and "Where's the Heat?" present fire and burn hazards. Children who have not had experience with fire are sometimes nervous with it and unsure of the dangers. Teach your children how to light matches safely and have them practice with you. "Explosion!," "Whack It!," and "Be a Swinger!" involve objects propelled at high speeds. Please read the directions for all of these activities and provide supervision to ensure safety.

Your help is also needed in collecting household, grocery, and pharmacy supplies. See page 6 for a list of materials. It can be frustrating to start an activity and then not have the needed materials handy. Help your child brainstorm reasonable substitutions when necessary.

Youngsters will have varying interest in the explanations at the back of the book. Ideally, they will pick up new vocabulary and concept understanding, yet, if they aren't interested at the moment, the concrete experience of simply *doing* the activities lays a valuable foundation for future abstractions.

Consider using activities in the book for gatherings of family members, neighbors, scouts, and others. The author hosted a mother-daughter group for such a science party. The girls did "Whirligig Rocketry" and "Fabulous Play Gloop" in one room while the moms did "Ramp" in another room. Then each group showed off what it had done and everyone had a great time. "Bubble Extravaganza," "Tall Tower," "Delicious Ice Cream," "Radiant Color," and "T-shirt Designs" also work well for group events.

Please share your discoveries, anecdotes, ideas, and jokes with the author at her website: http://www.countryday.net/science8/

Sighh

4

A Note to Teachers

There are many ways this book can be useful for you. Naturally, it could be a source of classroom activities. It could also:

- form the curriculum of a science elective
- provide plans for after-school science parties
- be a student sourcebook for a home science program within your curriculum

Suggestions for how to set up a science elective, run after-school parties, and develop a home science program are provided in the following discussion.

Since this book was written for both school and home use, the activities are written directly for the curious child. Measuring tools and other materials listed are those most likely to be available in the home. The decision to put English units before metric ones might offend your good teacher training. Sorry about that! The fact is that today more homes still use teaspoons than milliliters. Both English and metric units are given, so readers may choose the system they prefer.

Excitement and danger tend to go hand-in-hand. Therefore, some of the activities in this book have warnings. Specifically, the heat sources used in "Implosion!" and "Where's the Heat?" present fire and burn hazards. "Explosion!," "Whack It!," and "Be a Swinger!" involve objects propelled at high speeds. Please read the directions for all of these activities and provide for supervision to ensure safety.

Note that explanations are in the back of the book where they won't spoil the suspense of the activities. This way, students can make their own unbiased observations. Vocabulary terms are listed in the order the ideas are presented in the "What's Going On" concept explanations. Encourage recording sketches, cartoons, and other artwork along with the pure data. Many students make better connections with science content when their creative side is tapped. For example, though it takes an extra moment to turn an egg into "Your Dear Friend, Egbert," every student who does this remembers their Egbert. Take advantage of this!

To identify the science process skills in each activity, see the "National Science Education Standards Matrix" on page 158. To find activities that deal with specific science concepts see the "Physical Science Concept Index" on page 157.

Science Elective

If your school has electives in its schedule, you might like to develop a "Science Workshop" elective. Such a course can be as much fun for the teacher as the students. Choose hands-on activities that you love, and after the students have spent several days on a project, take time to reinforce the vocabulary and concepts that have come up. Then move on to a new project. Students in an elective can do activities that are too messy or too time consuming to use with every science student. The course can also be your testing ground for new ideas.

After-School Parties

Many of the activities in this book lend themselves well to optional 60–90 minute after-school party sessions for students who sign up in advance. Students of all ability levels are enthusiastic about such fun sessions. "Bubble Extravaganza," "Rainbow in a Drinking Straw," "Ramp," "Tall Tower," "Delicious Ice Cream," "Fabulous Play Gloop,"

"Radiant Color," and "T-shirt Designs" would be particularly good for this. Take some action photos of the students loving science during your parties and send them to the local newspaper.

Home Science

You can tie home science activities to your required curriculum. Most students appreciate having options about homework and enjoy assignments that are lab oriented. Assign activity choices one night a week or assign a particular activity when it relates to class curriculum. There is never enough lab time at school and taking advantage of home time will truly enrich your course. Require a brief record of time spent, activity done, and concepts learned. You may also want to have parents initial the record. For best parental support, send a letter home at the beginning of the program to explain the process. Assign credit based on time spent and choices made. For more information on a home science program called MOS, for "My Own Science," see the author's web site at http://www.countryday.net/science8/

Finally, enjoy using these materials with your students. Please share your feedback, anecdotes, ideas, and jokes with the author at her website:
http://www.countryday.net/science8/

Master List of Materials

Alka Seltzer or generic equivalent
Aluminum foil
Aluminum soft drink cans
Baking soda
Balloons, 4 or 5 inch
Balloons, 9 or 11 inch
Bathroom scale
Battery, 9 volt
Bowl
Bucket
Buzzer, 6–9 volts (from electronics store)
Candles
Cardboard tube
Citric acid
Cookie sheets
Coffee filters
Coffee mugs
Cooking oil
Cotton swabs
Cream of tartar
Cups, plastic

Cutting board
Duct tape
Eggs
Electric iron
Electric mixer
Elmer's Glue-All
Eye droppers, 4, glass (from pharmacy)
Food colors, 4
Fuji plastic film canisters
Funnels
Glasses, tall and clear
Glycerin (from pharmacy)
Golf ball
Greeting card and envelope
Hair blow dryer
Half and half cream product
Hammer
Hydrogen peroxide
Joy dishwashing soap
Kix cereal

Knife
Light stick
Marbles
Markers, permanent and washable
Matches, wooden
Matches, fireplace (extra long)
Needle or nail
Paper, copy
Pencil with eraser
Pennies
Pin
Ping-Pong ball
Pliers
Rope
Rubber bands
Rubbing alcohol
Ruler, plastic or wooden
Salt
Scissors
Soft drink bottles, plastic
Soup cans, 2

Spoons
Sta-Flo Liquid Starch
Stopwatch
Storage containers
String
Straws, regular and bendable
Sugar
Tape, cellophane
Thread
Tongs
Towels, paper
Tray, metal or plastic
Vanilla flavoring
Vinegar
Wire, 16–18 gauge
Yeast, dry
Zip top plastic bags

Optional
Hula-hoop
Karo syrup
Small plastic swimming pool
Thermometer

ACTIVITIES AND RECORD SHEETS

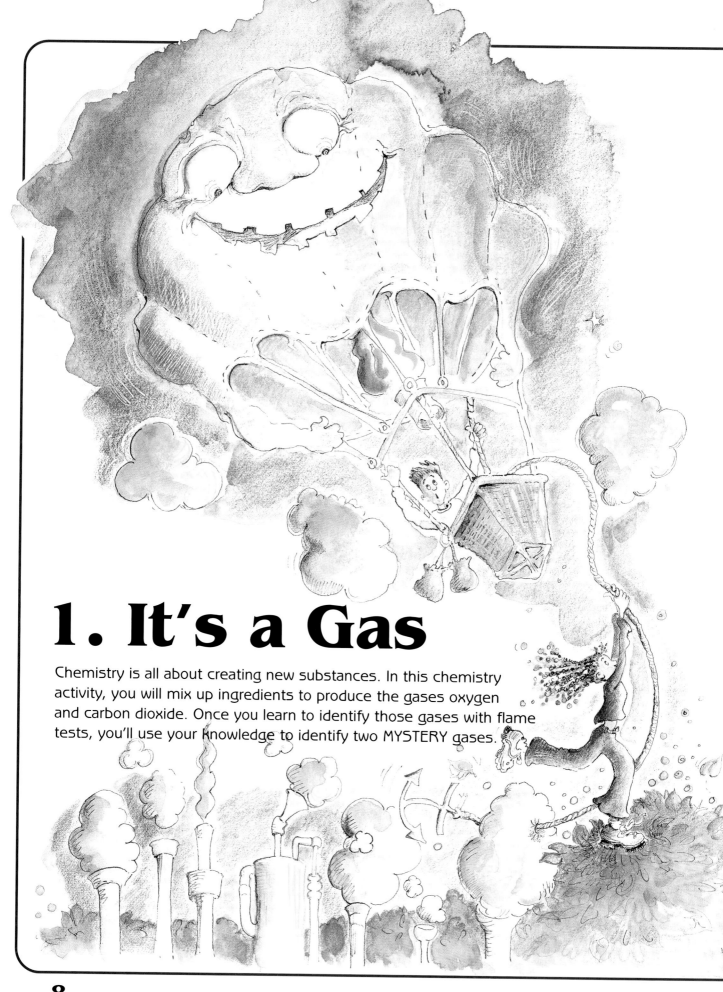

1. It's a Gas

Chemistry is all about creating new substances. In this chemistry activity, you will mix up ingredients to produce the gases oxygen and carbon dioxide. Once you learn to identify those gases with flame tests, you'll use your knowledge to identify two MYSTERY gases.

Materials

1 package of dry yeast
Several glasses or clear plastic cups
Hydrogen peroxide; 3% solution as found
   in pharmacies
12" fireplace matches or regular matches
   to light Popsicle sticks.

(Paper matches or wooden kitchen
matches alone are too short to be
safe in this activity.)
Vinegar
Baking soda
Alka Seltzer, 1 tablet
Sugar

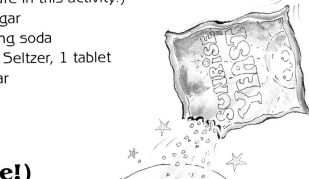

I. Oxygen (a personal favorite!)

1. Fill your cup one-fourth of the way with hydrogen peroxide.
2. Tear or cut the corner off the dry yeast package and
   sprinkle enough yeast to cover the surface of the liquid.
3. Swirl the cup.
4. What's happening?
5. Light a fireplace match, then hold the burning tip of it just
   above the liquid. Observe.
6. Blow out the flame on the stick. Hold the *glowing* tip just
   above the liquid. Observe. Repeat as often as you like.
7. Record your observations.

$\frac{1}{4}$ full

WARNING:

Lighting matches can
be dangerous. Adult
supervision is needed.

II. Carbon Dioxide

1. Fill a new cup one-fourth of the way with vinegar.
2. Add 1 teaspoon of baking soda.
3. What's happening?
4. Light a fireplace match and, once the foam is out of the way, hold the burning tip of it just above the liquid. Observe.
5. Light a new match. (Or use regular matches to relight remaining matchstick.) After it has burned several seconds, blow out the flame. Hold the glowing tip close to the liquid. Observe.
6. Record your observations.

III. Identifying Mystery Gases

You have just done a *flame test* and a *glowing splint test* for two known gases. Now do those same tests for unknown gases formed in other ways and try to identify the unknowns based on their test results.

Mystery Gas A

1. Fill a cup one-fourth of the way with warm (not hot) water.
2. Add 1 teaspoon (5 mL) sugar.
3. Add ½ teaspoon (2–3 mL) dry yeast and stir.
4. Cover the cup with a file card or a small plate.
5. Allow cup to sit undisturbed for about 30 minutes. Go on to *Mystery Gas B* while you wait.
6. Remove cover and swirl the cup to break up some of the bubbles.
7. Immediately do flame and glowing splint tests.
8. Record your observations and identify the gas.
9. You can repeat steps 5–7 all day or more. If you add sugar, you can keep the yeast solution going even longer.

> **Everything comes to him who hustles while he waits.**
> **—Thomas A. Edison**

Mystery Gas B

1. Fill a cup one-fourth of the way with water.
2. Add 1 Alka Seltzer tablet.
3. Do a flame test and a glowing splint test.
4. Record your observations.
5. Identify the gas.

Vocabulary and concepts appear on page 120.

Observations, Ideas, Sketches, Questions

TEST	OXYGEN	CARBON DIOXIDE	MYSTERY GAS A	MYSTERY GAS B
Flame Test Results:				
Glowing Splint Results:				
Identify Gas	Oxygen	Carbon Dioxide		

When a chemical reaction occurs, at least one _____ _____ is formed.

About 20% of the air we breathe is the gas called _____.

Q: What would you get if you crossed a hot air balloon with a ghost?
A: High spirits!

2. Explosion!

There is no fire hazard in this activity but you'll get a good "Bang!" out of it just the same. Depending on how far you decide to go, you could spend five minutes to five hours on this activity.

WARNING:
Keep your eyes out of the line of fire. Protective eyewear is recommended.

Materials

A few Fuji 35-millimeter plastic film cans. They are translucent white and the cap fits inside; the black kind will NOT work. Ask for them free of charge where film is developed.

3–30 Alka Seltzer tablets or a generic equivalent (the number depends on how enthusiastic you are!)

1 tray with sides

1 zip top plastic bag, pint to gallon size

I. Explosion!

1. How tolerant is your family of noise and splash? Consider the basement, garage, or outdoors for this activity.
2. Put water into the film can about one-third full. Set the can upright on the floor, on a tray to contain any mess.
3. Break an Alka Seltzer tablet in half.
4. Making sure you are not under a light and there are no other breakables nearby, put one half-tablet into the film can, close the lid tightly and *stand back!* (Stand at least 6 feet away.)
5. Record your results.

II. Explosion! Exploration

1. What can you learn about this? Here are some ideas for variations to get you started:
   a. What happens if you set the can on its lid?
   b. What if you lay the can on its side?
   c. What if you use ice water, or warm water, instead of water at room temperature?

d. Can you launch additional objects?

e. Is the time it takes for the cans to pop consistent?

f. What if you put the water and Alka Seltzer into a zip top bag instead of a film can?

g. What if you put the entire loaded film can into a zip top bag?

h. What if . . . .?

i. Can you . . . .?

2. Record your results on page 17.

III. Design Your Own Explosion! Experiment

There's a difference between messing around with an activity and doing a real experiment. An experiment has a clear purpose. The conditions are carefully controlled so that only one conditio (variable) is changed at a time. Measurements are taken and recorded and each step (trial) is repeated many times. In the end, the experiment and its results are published. If it is repeatable by other teams of experimenters, the conclusions gain further respect. In this way, knowledge about the world expands. While conclusions reached by this process aren't *always* correct, careful experiments are the best way we have to collect reliable information.

You can design your own experiment with Alka Seltzer. Look over the variations you tried and see which ones can be measured. You can measure time, temperature, weight, distance (including height), and amount (volume) of water or gas. If you are clever, you don't even need special measuring tools. For example, weight can be measured in units of pennies taped to the lid. Units of length can be floor tiles, and units of height can be flyswatter lengths or lengths of whatever is handy. For time, use a stop watch or a clock with a second hand.

*She **said** for MEASURING, got it?*

Worry is a futile thing, it's somewhat like a rocking chair.
   Although it keeps you occupied, it doesn't get you anywhere.
   —Anonymous

1. Design an experiment with a *purpose* that can be stated as follows: "What is the effect of _____ on _____?" For example, "What is *the effect of the weight of the cap* on *the height of cap flight?*" or "What is the effect of *the temperature of the water* on *the time before explosion?*"

2. Write a *procedure* describing how you will carry out the experiment. Writing this will help you think through the process. Number your steps as if you were writing the directions for someone else.

   Example: 1. Draw or scratch a mark about one-third of the way up the side of a film can and add water up to the line. 2. Use a flyswatter to measure how high the cap flies in an explosion using one tablet of Alka Seltzer. 3. Do two additional trials the same way. 4. Repeat step 2, with one penny taped to the top of the cap. Complete three explosion trials with one penny. 5. Repeat step 2, first using two pennies and then three pennies, with three trials of each.

3. Your *data* should be organized into a table something like this:

CAP "FLIGHT" HEIGHT (FLYSWATTER LENGTHS)

WEIGHT:	0 PENNIES	1 PENNY	2 PENNIES	3 PENNIES
Trial #1				
Trial #2				
Trial #3				
Average				

Notice that this sample data table calls for at least twelve explosions; three trials for each weight. For reliable results, you shouldn't do fewer, but you could add more pennies and/or do more trials of each number of pennies. You are limited only by your resources. Sometimes it may be time that limits you, sometimes materials, such as the number of Alka Seltzer tablets you have. Time, money, and availability of resources limit researchers in industry just as they limit you.

4. Let's say you've decided to look at the effect of cap weight on cap flight height. Be sure to keep all other conditions constant. Use the same temperature each time, measure the same amount of water each time, use consistent technique, and so on. Unplanned variations poison an experiment.

5. Before you really get going, do a few "shake down" trials to be sure that your systems are working well. It's difficult to accurately judge height, for example, and after the first couple trials you might decide to change your set-up. Maybe you decide to put the can on its side with its bottom next to a wall so the cap shoots out across the floor. If you change your setup, start your data collection over again.

6. Carry out your plan. Jot down things you observe during particular trials. An extra sheet is provided on page 18 for your experiment records.

7. Your *conclusion* goes after the data. It fulfills your purpose.

   Example: The greater the weight of the cap, the . . . .

8. Finally, invent a creative title that describes your experiment.

   Example: Flipping Your Lid; Does Weight Matter?

9. For some experiments, you may find that the factor you investigated had no effect at all. That is worth knowing! Some folks feel that such a result is disappointing, but it tells us just as much about the world as any other result, so hold your head high. Thomas Edison spent months of hard work trying to find the right material for the filament of his light bulb. He tried thousands of substances including metals of all kinds, coconut husks, leather, macaroni, fruit peels, cork, and hair. His outlook was that every material he tried taught him something and put him closer to his goal.

Keep in mind the features of a good experiment listed below. These features make your results more reliable than the results of casual exploration:

- Changing only one condition, or variable, at a time
- Using consistent technique and writing it down
- Measuring carefully
- Doing several trials for each set of conditions
- Making an organized, well labeled table of results (the data)

Should you make a graph? As long as at least one variable is measured, making a graph is an excellent way to show what your results really mean. If just one of the variables is measured, make a bar graph.

If *both* variables are measurements, then make a line graph.

See the "Graphing Appendix" on page 160 for more information on graphing.

Vocabulary and concepts appear on page 121.

Q: Why didn't the skeleton cross the road?
A: He had no guts!

Observations, Ideas, Sketches, Questions

MESSING AROUND

THINGS I WILL TRY	PREDICTED RESULT	ACTUAL RESULT

Explosion! Experiment Report

Title:

Purpose:

Diagram and Explanation of Set-Up:

Data Table:

Other Observations:

Graph: (See next page)
Conclusion:

Explosion! Graph

3. Implosion!

You'll have to drink up some soda pop (anything for the sake of science, right?) to get prepared for this activity. Then see how calm your nerves are when the soda can goes "POP!"

WARNING: You will be working with a stove burner and boiling water, both of which can cause serious burns. Have an adult help you and be careful not to touch hot surfaces!

Materials

Several empty aluminum soft drink cans
Kitchen stove burner, gas or electric
Bowl of ice water
A pair of tongs that will securely hold the can
(try it) or a good oven mitt with thumb

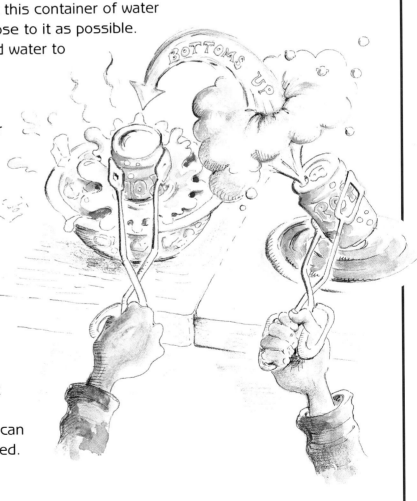

I. Implosion!

1. Add 1 generous tablespoon (20 mL) of water
   to an empty soft drink can.
2. Place the can on the stove burner while the burner is
   "off." (If you have a gas stove that has grate supports that
   are too far apart to hold the can properly, get help from an
   adult before you continue.)
3. Place the bowl, nearly full of ice water, right next to the
   stove. If you are right handed, put this container of water
   to the left of the burner and as close to it as possible.
   If you are left handed, put the cold water to
   the right of the burner.
4. Turn on the burner and heat the
   can. Once you see steam rising
   from the can, continue heating for
   one more minute.
5. Think this next part through and
   practice it before you do it. You
   are going to get a good grip on
   the can near its bottom, with
   the tongs held so that your
   hand is *palm up*. In *one
   swift motion* you are going
   to lift the can off the
   burner, turn it over, and
   place it, top down, in the
   cold water. Practice the motion
   with an extra can so you can do it
   without hesitation.
6. When you are ready, turn the hot can
   over into the water as you practiced.

7. You jumped, didn't you! *Turn off the burner.*
8. Record your observations, including a sketch of the can before and after its dunking on the record sheet.
9. Repeat the above steps with new cans to try to achieve the most impressive result.

WARNING: *Never* heat a closed container.

Keep smiling . . . It makes everyone wonder what you're up to.

II. Investigate Implosion!

1. To find out the effect of various conditions, try changing one condition at a time in the steps above. Here are a few questions you might try to answer. Make a prediction before you begin each investigation.
   a. What is the effect of waiting a few seconds after taking the can from the heat before putting it in the water?
   b. What is the effect of putting the can right-side-up in the water?
   c. What is the effect of using an empty can instead of one with a little water in it?
   d. What is the effect of _____?
      (Think of your own question.)
   e. Record your results on the record sheet.
2. Using what you have learned from your investigations, write your hypothesis (educated guess) of why the can behaves the way it does.

Vocabulary and concepts appear on page 122.

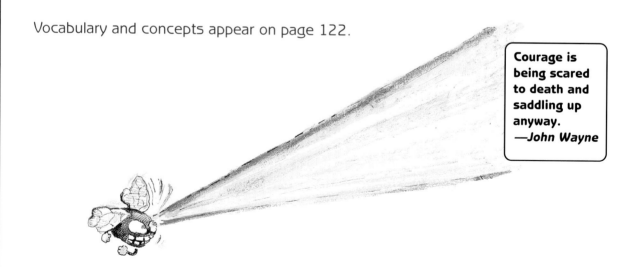

Courage is being scared to death and saddling up anyway.
—John Wayne

Observations, Ideas, Sketches, Questions

Soft Drink Can Before: **After:**

Condition Changed	Predicted Result	Actual Result

Hypothesis:

4. Instant Meringue

Egg whites can be whipped into a nice, white foam when beaten several minutes with an electric mixer set on high. In this activity, you will get the same effect in about 10 seconds. No mixer required!

Materials

1 clear plastic cup; 8- or 12-ounce size
1 or 2 eggs
Baking soda
1 small bowl
Powdered citric acid; vitamin C tablets
    or Sour Salt
A hammer or a mortar and pestle
    to grind tablets
Paper towel or cloth napkin

> Manners are a sensitive awareness of the feelings of others. If you have that awareness, you have good manners, no matter what fork you use.
>
> —*Emily Post*

I. Instant Meringue

1. Grind up enough vitamin C to make 1 teaspoon (5 mL) of powder. You can wrap the tablets in two layers of paper towel and gently hammer them on a concrete floor or chopping board. Or you can grind them with a mortar and pestle.

2. Separate the yolk from the white of 1 egg: Hit the middle of the egg against the side of the bowl to crack it, then hold the egg upright over the bowl and lift off the top half of the shell. Much of the white will fall into the bowl when you do this. Then pour the unbroken yolk from shell to shell, letting the rest of the egg white dribble into the bowl. Should the yolk break and get mixed with the white, start over with another egg and a clean bowl. The greatest of chefs had to learn this skill just as you have!

egg white only

3. Put 1 tablespoon (15 mL) water, 1 teaspoon (5 mL) egg white, and 1 teaspoon (5 mL) baking soda into the cup and stir them.

4. Sprinkle 1 teaspoon (5 mL) of citric acid powder into the cup and *vigorously* swirl the cup to the count of 10. Turn the cup upside down. Voilà! You are too clever! Go find someone to show off for. You should have enough egg white from one egg to repeat your foam creation about three more times.

II. Investigate Instant Meringue

As long as you use food substances, it is safe to investigate changes in your meringue recipe. What if you use twice as much egg white? What if you use flour instead of baking soda? What if you add a teaspoon of sugar? What if you use lemon juice instead of citric acid? What if . . . ? Decide on changes you want to try, then write predictions of the effect each will have before you actually try them. Volume (amount), color, and texture are some of the different results you might look for. The best way to judge results is to add all but the final ingredient to several cups, writing on the outside with a marker what is different about each one. Make only *one* change to each cup so that it is clear what caused any new result. One by one, add the final ingredient, swirl, and record your findings. The cup with the original recipe is the control that you compare to all others. Repeat any trials you question. Think about and write what you've learned by your investigation under "Conclusions."

Vocabulary and concepts appear on page 124.

Observations, Ideas, Sketches, Questions

I. Observations:

Doctor: How did you get here so fast?
Patient: Flu.

II. Investigations:

RECIPE CHANGE	PREDICTED RESULT	ACTUAL RESULT

Conclusions:

5. Your Dear Friend, Egbert

Play along with this fun activity for insight into density, buoyancy, and solutions.

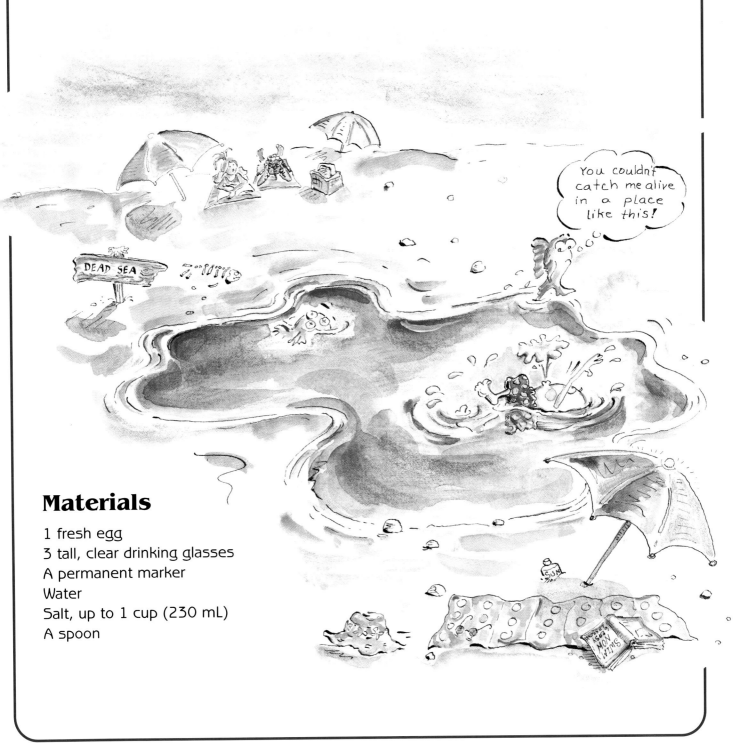

Materials

1 fresh egg
3 tall, clear drinking glasses
A permanent marker
Water
Salt, up to 1 cup (230 mL)
A spoon

I. Egbert's Adventures

1. Use the permanent marker to carefully transform your plain egg into your dear friend Egbert (or Egbertina perhaps?). You will be taking him on some swimming adventures. Because he is an egg, swim trunks are optional.

2. Turn one of the tall glasses into a swimming

← 1 inch (3 cm)

> I can't say I was ever lost, but I was bewildered once for three days.
> —*Daniel Boone*

pool for Egbert using fresh tap water. Carefully add Egbert to the water in the glass. Sketch his "swimming" behavior in this pool on the record sheet. (O.K., he can't really *swim*, but we won't let on we notice.)

3. When you think he's had enough, remove Egbert from the pool, using a spoon.

4. Now, you and Egbert go on a vacation to the very salty Dead Sea. Take the second glass and put salt in the bottom *at least* 1 inch (3 cm) deep. Add water until the glass is about two-thirds full and stir. Help Egbert into the Dead Sea water and see how he likes swimming there. Sketch him in the Dead Sea. If Egbert's behavior is *not* different here than in the fresh water, stir in more salt until it is.

5. Egbert likes swimming in the Dead Sea so much that he insists you bring home Dead Sea water for your backyard swimming pool.

6. Now you are back home and Egbert is anxious to swim. In the third glass, make a new batch of Dead Sea water by repeating Step 4 *except* stop adding water when the glass is about half full. Place him in the glass.

7. What's this? Your next door neighbor just turned on her lawn sprinkler and the water is coming over the fence into Egbert's pool. Slowly and gently dribble fresh tap water down the inside wall of the glass on top of the salt water until the glass is almost full. Sketch Egbert swimming now.

8. Bring him out with a spoon when he's ready without stirring the pool and allow him to lounge poolside. (If the sun comes out you may need to get him his sunglasses.) Now see if you can find Egbert some swim buddies. You will use all three swimming areas that you have prepared to test for swimming buddies.

II. The Search for Egbert's Swim Buddies

1. Collect and test objects from around the house to try to find six or seven objects that will behave just like Egbert in all three of the glasses. Try toy pieces, an eraser, a bottle cap, various foods, and so on. Place them in each container and observe how they behave. Use a spoon to fish them back out of the glasses and record your results in the space on the observations page. Be careful not to stir the water in glass #3. If an object matches Egbert's behavior in each glass, it's a good swim buddy.

Vocabulary and concepts appear on page 124.

Observations, Ideas, Sketches, Questions

Draw in Egbert.

Fresh Water

Salt Water

Salt/Fresh Water

Nursery notice: All babies subject to change without notice.

Object	Float or Sink in Fresh Water?	Float or Sink in Salt Water?	Float or Sink in Salt/Fresh Water?	A Buddy?

6. Rainbow in a Drinking Straw

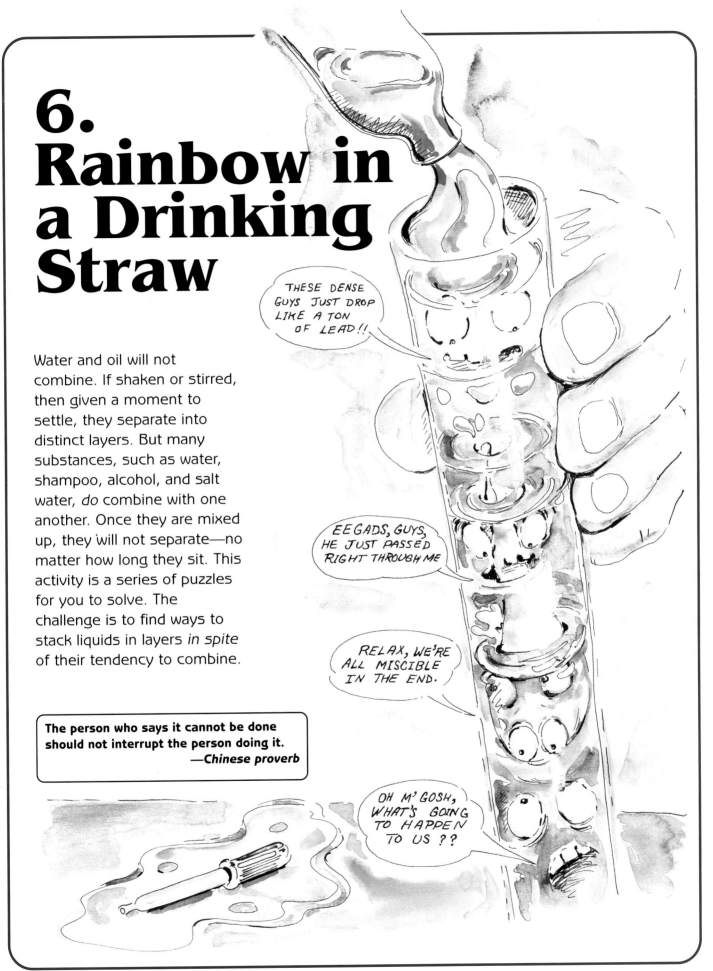

Water and oil will not combine. If shaken or stirred, then given a moment to settle, they separate into distinct layers. But many substances, such as water, shampoo, alcohol, and salt water, *do* combine with one another. Once they are mixed up, they will not separate—no matter how long they sit. This activity is a series of puzzles for you to solve. The challenge is to find ways to stack liquids in layers *in spite* of their tendency to combine.

> **The person who says it cannot be done should not interrupt the person doing it.**
> **—Chinese proverb**

Materials

3–4 clear drinking straws
A paper clip
4 eye droppers, any type.
  You will need *glass* droppers
  for Pop Bottle Magic
  (available in pharmacies)
Food coloring; four colors
Several cotton swabs

Water
Rubbing alcohol
Shampoo
Salt
4 small cups
4 coffee mugs
A friend
Vegetable oil, optional
Karo syrup, optional

The Big Picture

Once you have prepared four colored solutions, you are going to add a bit of each to a miniature test tube made from a drinking straw to solve a puzzle. The challenge is to find sequences of the four solutions such that each solution will stay separate from the solution above and below. We'll call this "stacking." In "Substance Stacking," you will try to stack four different substances. In "Concentration Stacking," you will try to stack four different concentrations of the same solution. In "Temperature Stacking," you will try to stack water at four different temperatures.

I. Substance Stacking

1. Set out 4 small cups each with about 1 tablespoon (15 mL) of one of the following:
   Shampoo
   Rubbing alcohol
   Water
   Salt water made with
       1/4 teaspoon (1 mL) salt
       in 1/4 cup (60 mL) water

2. Add and stir into each cup two drops of food coloring as follows: shampoo: blue; alcohol: green; water: yellow; and salt water: red. To keep the solutions pure, assign a different dropper to stir each cup, and keep using only the proper dropper.

3. Make a miniature test tube out of a drinking straw by folding the straw 1 inch (2–3 cm) from the end and then folding it once more and clamping the folded part with a paper clip.

4. While you hold the straw at an angle, use a dropper to add several drops of a substance to your "test tube." (The shampoo is going to be slow moving so be patient.) If the tube gets blocked with trapped air, pinch it a few times to release the air. Let the solution dribble down the side of the straw.

5. Using the proper dropper, add a second substance to your test tube. It may stack above the first or it may move down through it and blend. Whatever occurs, record the sequence you added on a blank tube on the record sheet and show the result on the side, as shown.

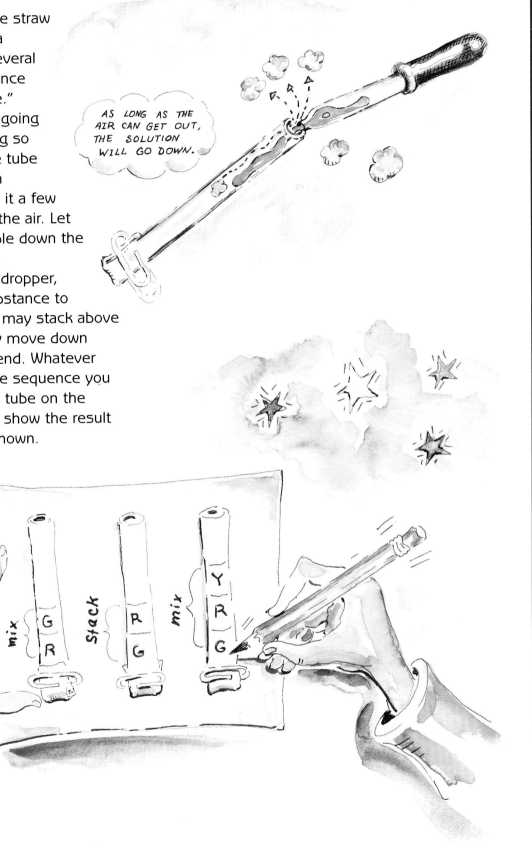

6. Empty your straw between tries by taking off the paper clip and rinsing with water. You can do this right at the faucet or by dipping the straw several times into a pitcher of water. Tap excess water out of the straw and dry it further using a cotton swab so that you start with an almost dry tube each time.

7. Using both trial and error and logic, continue adding combinations of the four substances until you find a sequence in which all four will stack. When you do discover one such series, try it again to make sure it is repeatable.

8. Once you've confirmed one sequence, see how many more four-layer sequences you can get to stack. You might like to use crayons or markers to color your record of successful sequences. Did you solve the puzzle? Looks neat, doesn't it?

9. Label and set aside a nicely stacked sample to watch over the next few hours and days.

II. Concentration Stacking

1. Again use four cups. Label them "a," "b," "c," and "d." This time you will prepare different solutions as follows. Measure carefully and stir:

    a. 1/2 cup (120 mL) water

    b. 1/2 cup (120 mL) water and 1/8 teaspoon (0.5 mL) salt

    c. 1/2 cup (120 mL) water and 1/2 teaspoon (2 mL) salt

    d. 1/2 cup (120 mL) water and 1 heaping teaspoon (6 mL) salt

2. If possible, have a friend color these solutions four different colors so you don't know which is which. If all the cups do not look the same, your friend should mix these up as well. Have your friend keep a secret record of which color goes with which lettered solution.

3. Now for the puzzle. By trial and error, find sequences that will stack. Record your results. When you find one sequence that works, repeat it, then look for more.

4. Label and set aside a nicely stacked sample to watch over the next few hours and days.

III. Temperature Stacking

This time, use coffee mugs or similar containers for a full cup of each solution. The four solutions are all going to be colored water. Only the temperature will differ from cup to cup.

1. Make one mug of ice water. Color it blue.
2. Put room temperature water in the next mug. Color it green.
3. Run the hot water faucet until the water feels warm and put that in the next mug. Color it yellow.
4. Run the water longer until it is quite hot and put that into the fourth mug. Color it red.
5. Make a prediction about a stackable sequence.
6. Again, search for stacking sequences. Use enough of each solution so that you use all the available space in the straw. Realize that color boundaries will be less distinct than they may have been with the other two stacking activities. They should still be repeatable.
7. Record your results.
8. Label and set aside a nicely stacked sample to watch over the next few hours and days.
9. Put all labeled samples out where you will notice them several times a day. What happens to them?

IV. Exploration Ideas

1. Try stacking other food liquids and solutions. Don't use household cleaning products as some of them interact to make poisonous gas. Record your results.
2. Try any or all of the three stacking procedures presented earlier using a larger container such as a drinking glass instead of a straw. Record your results.
3. You can make a terrific stacked column in a tall glass that will last for weeks using Karo syrup first, then water, cooking oil, and rubbing alcohol. Color all but the oil, then add them, one at a time, to a tall glass or jar. Don't let the water and alcohol make contact or they will blend permanently.

Vocabulary and concepts appear on page 126.

Observations, Ideas, Sketches, Questions

Solution Stacking:

Prediction: _____

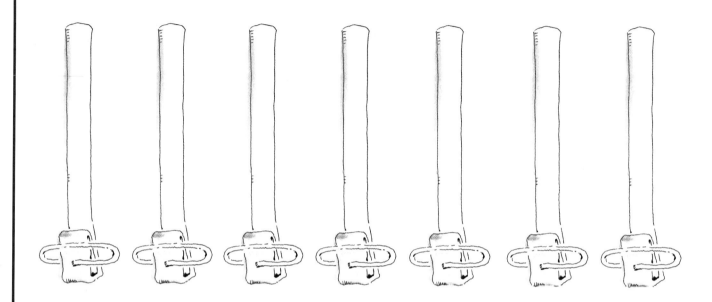

Concentration Stacking:

Prediction: _____

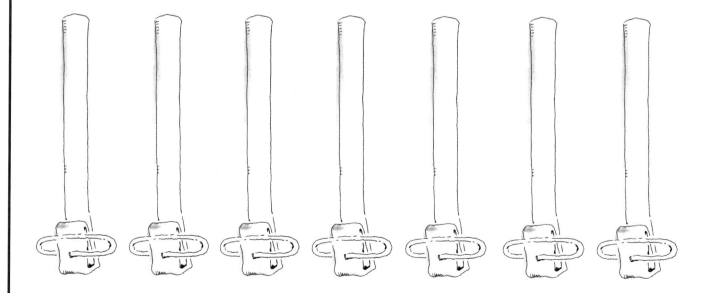

Temperature Stacking:

Prediction: _____

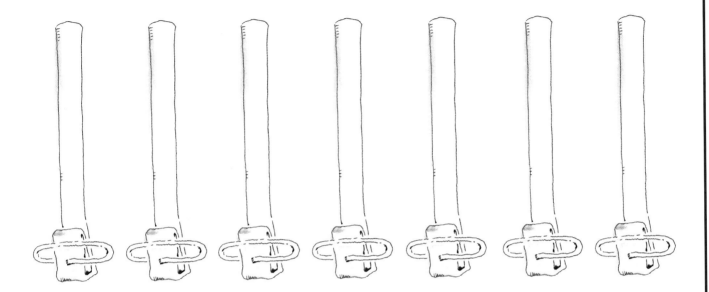

Exploration Observations:

Every time I get on a ferry it makes me cross.

7. Ice and Oil:

Would Icebergs Have Been a Problem If the *Titanic* Had Sailed on Oil?

SEE MOLLY ?!

You've probably noticed that ice cubes, like icebergs, always float in water. Maybe you've also noticed that oil floats on water or you've read that when an oil tanker causes a spill, the oil spreads out on top of the water. So what do you think about *ice* with *oil*? Would the ice float or the oil? Hmmm....

Write your prediction on the record sheet ("Observations, Ideas . . .).

Now find out. But that's not all to this activity. Something else very interesting will happen that should not be given away in advance.

Materials

Tall, slim, clear container such as a tall
    drinking glass or olive jar
Vegetable oil
Food coloring (optional)
Ice cube tray or small paper cup
Water
A spoon

Which Floats, Ice or Oil?

1. Make a colored ice cube by mixing 2 drops of food coloring with water in a tiny paper cup or in a compartment of a regular ice cube tray. It takes a few hours to freeze water in your freezer, so do this in advance. The ice you make will need to fit easily into the clear glass container. If you don't have time to make the colored ice, regular ice will work. It just doesn't look as good.
2. Pour oil into the glass up to about 1 inch (2 or 3 cm) from the top.
3. Make *sure* you made your prediction on the record sheet.
4. Now, gently add your colored (or clear) ice cube to the oil with a spoon. You don't want the oil to splash.
5. Does the ice float or sink? Record your observations on the record sheet.
6. That was just the beginning. Now watch a while. Something else is going to happen. It may take a few minutes.
7. Make a sketch of what you see in the space on the record sheet. Show in your sketch the shape the water from the melting ice takes. Cool, huh?
8. Below your sketch, try to explain why the ice, the oil, and the melted ice behave the way they do.
9. What other situations can you think of where matter forms naturally into spheres?

Vocabulary and concepts appear on page 127.

Observations, Ideas, Sketches, Questions

Prediction: _____

Sketch:

> Wise man says:
> When in doubt,
> mumble.

Explanation:

_____

_____

_____

_____

_____

Ice _____ in oil.

Water _____ in oil.

FISHSICKLES
$1.25
ALL NATURAL
LAKE FROZEN!

8. Pop Bottle Magic

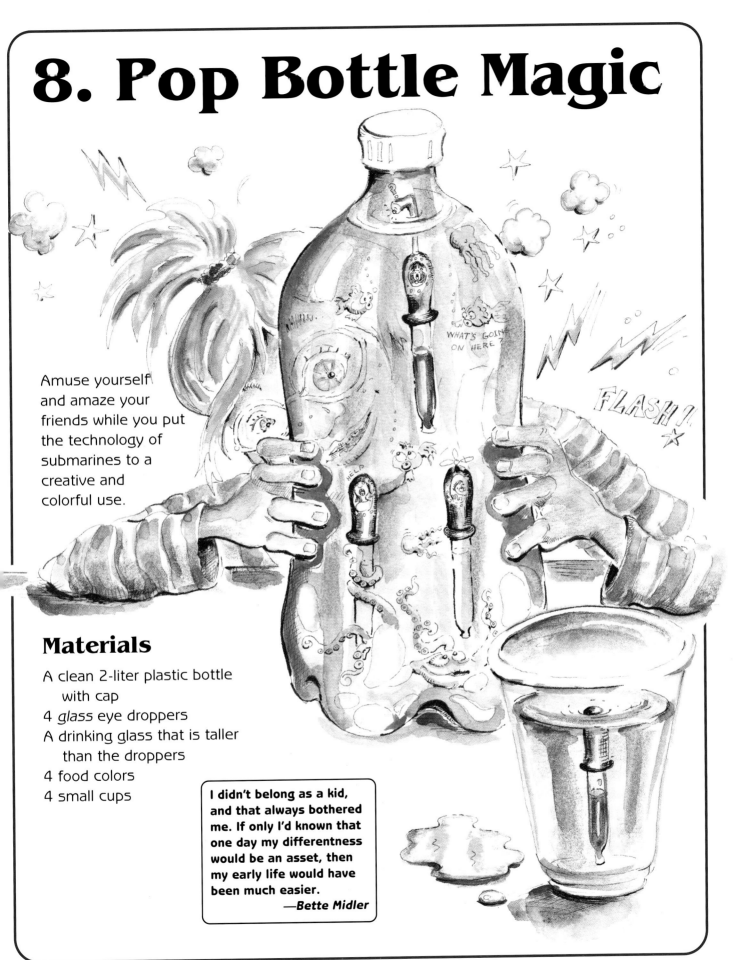

Amuse yourself and amaze your friends while you put the technology of submarines to a creative and colorful use.

Materials

A clean 2-liter plastic bottle with cap
4 *glass* eye droppers
A drinking glass that is taller than the droppers
4 food colors
4 small cups

> I didn't belong as a kid, and that always bothered me. If only I'd known that one day my differentness would be an asset, then my early life would have been much easier.
> —Bette Midler

I. Magic Finger

1. Fill the drinking glass nearly to the top with water. Prepare one eye dropper as follows:
2. Draw water from the glass into the dropper by pinching, then releasing, the dropper bulb while the glass tip is under water.
3. Put the dropper into the water in the drinking glass and see how it behaves. You want it to float, but just barely. Adjust the amount of water in the dropper until the tip of the bulb just breaks the surface of the water when it floats.
4. Fill the 2-liter bottle nearly to the top with water.
5. Without squeezing the dropper you prepared, move it from the glass to the bottle.
6. Put the bottle cap on snugly.
7. Squeeze the sides of the bottle and watch what happens to the dropper. (If you have to squeeze very hard to get a reaction from the dropper, start over. Remove the dropper from the bottle by overfilling the bottle at the sink so that the dropper will float out the opening. Add a little more water to the dropper, then return it to the nearly full bottle.)
8. To turn this dropper action into a magic trick, practice squeezing the bottle with one hand, while you focus on the other hand as a pointer. Make it look as though your pointer finger is directing the action of the dropper. Add commands like "Sink!," "Stop!," and "Rise!" With practice, you can develop very good control.

9. As you practice, watch the dropper and the water in it closely. See if you can figure out why they behave this way. Record your observations and any hypotheses you might have about why they do what they do.

10. Practice the magic in a mirror, then search out an audience.

II. Obedient Colors

This time, you will set up 4 droppers, each with a slightly different amount of different colors of water.

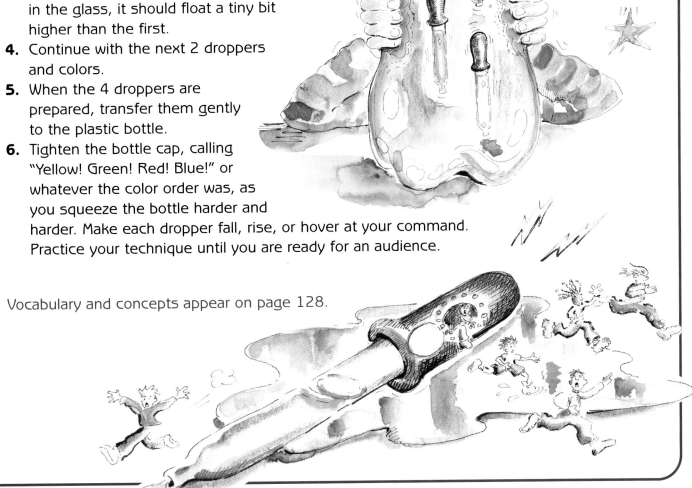

1. Prepare bright samples of 4 colors of water in the small cups by adding several drops of food color to water.

2. Draw colored water into the first dropper. As before, place the dropper in the glass of clear water to check that the dropper just *barely* floats.

3. Put slightly less of a different colored water into the next dropper. When the dropper is placed in the glass, it should float a tiny bit higher than the first.

4. Continue with the next 2 droppers and colors.

5. When the 4 droppers are prepared, transfer them gently to the plastic bottle.

6. Tighten the bottle cap, calling "Yellow! Green! Red! Blue!" or whatever the color order was, as you squeeze the bottle harder and harder. Make each dropper fall, rise, or hover at your command. Practice your technique until you are ready for an audience.

Vocabulary and concepts appear on page 128.

Observations, Ideas, Sketches, Questions

Observations of dropper:

Q. What do you get if you cross a canary and a magician?
A. Cheep tricks!

Your hypothesis of why it works:

Draw a cartoon?

9. Bernoulli's Blast I:

Give Me a Lift

> A journey of a thousand miles must begin with a single step.
> —*Chinese proverb*

Daniel Bernoulli, a Swiss mathematician and physicist, figured out the air pressure phenomenon responsible for *lift* on airplane wings. Here is a fascinating example of lift followed by a puzzle for you to solve. Try to stay in control while your materials get carried away!

Materials

1 drinking straw
1 glass of water, filled nearly to the top
1 Ping-Pong ball
2 small cups 2–3 inches (5–8 cm) tall
Tape, masking or cellophane

I. Plant Sprayer

1. Cut the straw in half.
2. Put half of the straw into the glass of water.
3. Use the other half of the straw to send a hard, sharp burst of air across the top of the first. If nothing interesting happens, you didn't blow hard enough. Try again.
4. Go to a mirror and watch what the water in the first straw does when you blow across the top straw.
5. Record your observations with a sketch. Do you have a hypothesis on why the water acts as it does?
6. Use your results to help you solve the Ping-Pong Puzzler below.

II. Ping-Pong Puzzler

Challenge I: Get the Ping-Pong ball out of a small cup that is *taped to the table*. The cup, with only the ball in it, is to be upright and may *not* be touched. You also may *not* touch the ball with any solid or liquid object.

Record your solution. If you are having trouble, realize that you are surrounded by hints. Think! Reread!

Challenge II: Get the Ping-Pong ball out of the first small cup and into the second small cup that is placed about 4 inches (10 cm) away. Both cups are to be upright and taped to the table. Again, neither the cups nor the ball may be touched by any solid or liquid.

Record your solution. How many tries before success? This challenge would make a good party game, don't you think?

III. Lift Investigations

What else can you get to lift? Wads of tissue paper? Bubbles?
What if you blow bubbles in the back seat of the car while riding with one window open. Does the speed of the car affect the behavior of the bubbles? Make a prediction before you try it.

Vocabulary and concepts appear on page 129.

Observations, Ideas, Sketches, Questions

Plant Sprayer Observations:

Q: Where does King Arthur keep his armies?
A: In his sleevies.

Plant Sprayer Hypothesis?

Ping-Pong Puzzler I:

Ping-Pong Puzzler II:

Results of Investigations:

WHAT I WILL TRY	PREDICTED RESULT	ACTUAL RESULT

10. Bernoulli's Blast II:
No Visible Means of Support

You can use Bernoulli's Principle to make a Ping-Pong ball or a piece of cereal hover in thin air. It looks like magic!

> Nothing great was ever achieved without enthusiasm.
> —*Ralph Waldo Emerson*

Materials for Hovering Ping-Pong Ball

1 electric blow dryer
1 Ping-Pong ball
Permanent markers

Materials for Hovering Cereal Ball

1 bendable drinking straw
Ball-shaped cereal such as
   Kix or Cocoa Puffs

Materials for Funnel Blast

A clean funnel with a narrow
   stem or a wide stemmed
   funnel, a straw, and a
   paper towel
1 Ping-Pong ball

I. Hovering Ping-Pong Ball

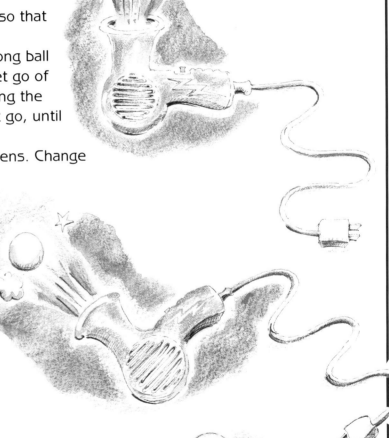

1. Use markers to draw a colorful design on the Ping-Pong ball.
2. Hold the blow dryer set on low speed so that the moving air is going straight up.
3. With your other hand, hold the Ping-Pong ball a few inches above the nozzle, then let go of the ball. Try this several times, adjusting the distance from the nozzle when you let go, until the ball will just hover. WOW!
4. Try a higher speed and see what happens. Change the speed back and forth.
5. Try tilting the dryer slightly to one side. See how far you can tilt the dryer without losing the ball. Bernoulli would be proud of you!
6. Record your observations.

This amazing feat can be scaled down using a cereal ball and a bendable straw.

II. Hovering Cereal

1. Choose a nice, round piece of cereal.
2. Bend the straw to a right angle (90°) and put it in your mouth like a pipe.
3. Take a deep breath, then, with the cereal held above the straw opening, *gently* and *with control*, blow air at the cereal. Let go of the cereal once you start blowing.

4. This takes practice! Adjust the force of the air you exhale. If you still have trouble, try different pieces of cereal. You can get the knack with practice, but don't overdo. Stop if you start to feel dizzy or out of breath and try again later.

5. Record your observations.

Keeping a ball up this way is one thing. But now, here's a Bernoulli Blast where the air blows downward, yet, like magic, the ball *still* stays up!

III. Funnel Blast

1. If your funnel has a stem that is greater than 1/2 inch (1 cm) in diameter, narrow the opening by wrapping the end of half a straw with paper towel until the toweling fits snugly into the funnel stem. Now the straw acts as the stem of the funnel.

2. Bend your head down so that you will be able to blow through the funnel straight down toward the floor.

3. Hold the Ping-Pong ball inside the funnel right up close to the hole.

4. After a deep breath, blow through the narrow end of the funnel with a burst of air and continue to exhale for 1 second. What happens to the ball?

5. Record your observations.

Want to go farther? With adult supervision you can scale UP the blow dryer demonstration with a beach ball and an industrial shop vacuum set on reverse. Choose a ball according to the power of the vacuum's fan. The vacuum hose and wand may be held for a single demonstration, or mounted for a continuous display. This is a mesmerizing attraction for a festival, party, or science fair.

Vocabulary and concepts appear on page 132.

Observations, Ideas, Sketches, Questions

Hovering Ping-Pong Ball:

**Maximum Dryer Angles
(degrees from vertical):**

High speed: _____

Medium: _____

Low: _____

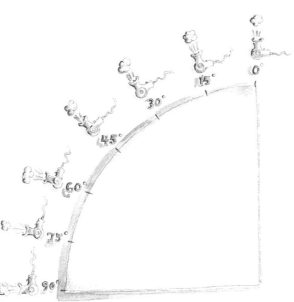

Hovering Cereal:

Describe the best technique:

Q: How did Frankenstein's monster win the election?
A: I guess he got all the volts!

Funnel Blast:

11. Radiant Color

Are you an artist? In this activity, even the least artistic soul will create striking disks of color. You may learn a few interesting facts, as well, about capillary action, solubility, and the use of chromatography in detective work.

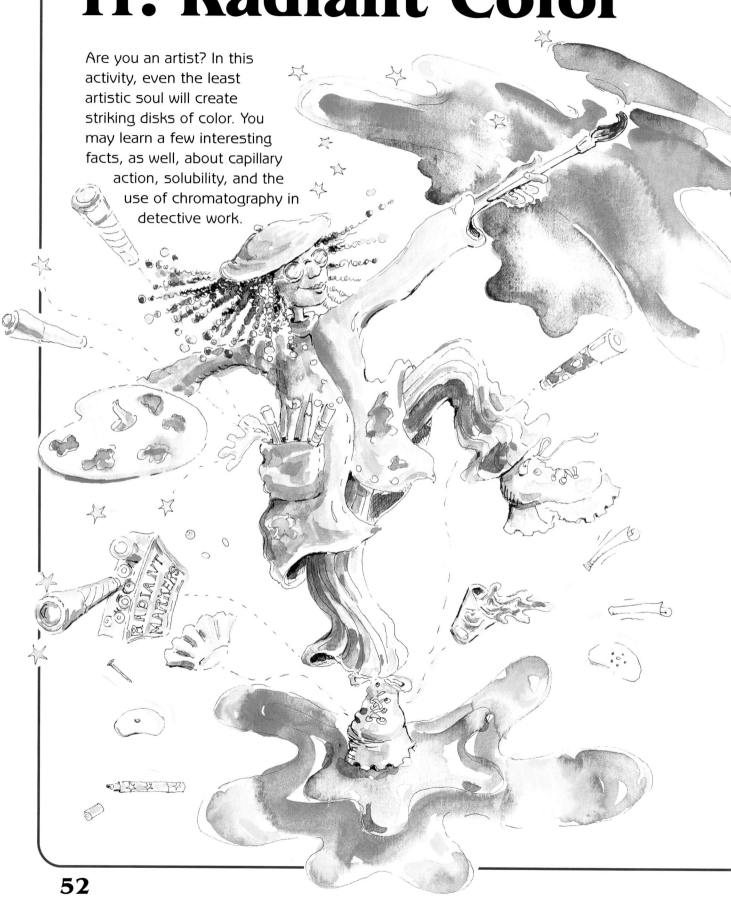

Materials

2 or 3 small cups
Coffee filters; flat bottomed,
  any size
Scissors
1 dime or penny

Washable markers in several
  colors, including black
1 ballpoint pen or nail
Food coloring

I. Radiant Color

1. Fill a small glass three-fourths full with water.
   Dry the rim.
2. Cut out the circular bottom of a coffee filter.
   Set the wavy-edge piece aside.
3. Place the dime in the center of the circular paper and draw spots or dashes around
   it with *one* washable marker.
4. Wave the paper in the air to dry the ink. Apply a second coat of marker ink to each
   dot or dash with the same pen as before.
5. Cut a section from the edge you set aside and roll it into a skinny cone as shown.

6. Remove the dime and poke a hole about 1/4 inch in diameter (0.5
   cm) in the center of the paper circle with a ballpoint pen, nail, or other
   round, sharp object.
7. Push the pointed end of the cone up from below, far enough into the hole
   so that it will stay. In a moment, you will set the filter paper on top of the
   glass of water. The paper cone will extend down into the water
   and act like a wick. Make a prediction of what will happen when
   you do this. Record your prediction on the record sheet.
8. Go ahead and place the filter paper with cone on the cup. You can
   run several papers at once in different cups using different pen
   colors for each.
9. Wait and watch. It may take 5–10 minutes for the water
   to fully develop your marks. Isn't that cool? When you
   want to stop the process, just pick up the paper, take out
   the wick, and set the paper out to dry.
10. Record your observations.

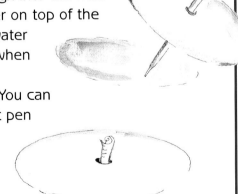

II. Radiant Color Exploration

What questions will you investigate?

What color bands result from other pen colors treated this way? Be sure to try black.

What if you let the paper sit on the cup for an hour or longer?

How do similar colors of different brands of pen compare?

How could you use this process to identify the brand of an unlabeled ink sample?

Does food coloring separate into different colors? (Apply food coloring with the tip of a toothpick dipped into the color.)

What if you mix some food colors together first?

How do other shapes of colored marks such as stars or triangles react to spreading?

What is the effect of the shape of the paper?

Does the water temperature affect how long the spreading takes?

What other types of paper or fabric can be used for this?

What designs can you create with this process?

Make predictions before each new effort.

Record your observations. Record also any hypotheses you have about why the colors behave as they do.

III. Radiant Color Experiment

Pick one of the exploration possibilities to complete as a real experiment. Construct your report on the form on page 57. The finished filter paper with colors separated is called a *chromatogram* (a color picture).

1. Write a *purpose* in the form: What is the effect of _____ on _____? What goes in the blanks are called the *variables*.

> **Example:** What is the effect of *the brand of black pen* on *chromatograms made with them?*

2. Write a *procedure* describing how you will carry out the experiment. Writing this will help you think through the process. Number your steps as if you were writing the directions for someone else.

Example:
1. Find 3 different brands of washable black markers.
2. Use pencil to label the edge of each of 9 filter papers with the name of the brands, one name to each of three papers.
3. Apply 6 dots of ink from the proper marker in a circle around the centers of the papers.
4. Add holes in the centers, add wicks, and set the papers on cups of water until most of the filter paper is wet. Remove.
5. Allow all to dry and compare them.
6. Staple the chromatograms to paper in three groups and label them clearly.

3. Your *data* section is your labeled display of chromatograms along with any measurements or any other observations you may have made.

4. Your *conclusion* goes after the data. It fulfills your purpose.

> **Example:** The Brand X black marker separates into brown, rust, dark blue, and turquoise. The Brand Y black marker separates into gray, brown, black, and turquoise. The Brand Z black marker separates into bright shades of pink, green, and turquoise. The black inks start out looking the same, but each separates into a distinct chromatogram.

5. Finally, invent a creative *title* that partially describes your experiment.

> **Example:** X,Y,Z: Are All Brands Created Equal?

You can do many different experiments with this process, which is called *chromatography*. Keep in mind the features of a good experiment listed below. These features make your results more reliable than the results of casual exploration:

- Careful labeling
- Doing several trials for each set of conditions
- Changing only one condition, or variable, at a time
- Using consistent technique and writing it down
- Making an organized display of results (the data)

Should you make a graph? That all depends on the kind of data you collect. Most of the experiment ideas involved data collected directly with the senses without measurements or numbers. This kind of data, called *qualitative*, cannot be graphed. However, for experiments where the data for one or both variables can be put on a number line, a graph is very helpful in showing the meaning of the numbers. If the data for just one of the variables can be put on a number line, make a bar graph.

If the data for *both* variables can be put on a number line, then a line graph should be done.

For more information on making graphs, see the "Graphing Appendix" on page 160.

Vocabulary and concepts appear on page 134.

Sample Bar Graph
THE DISTANCE THE LEADING COLOR TRAVELED IN 2 MINUTES FOR EACH BRAND

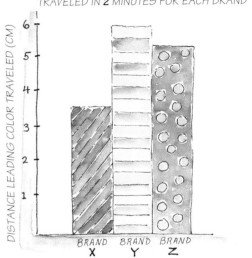

Sample Line Graph
THE EFFECT OF WATER TEMPERATURE ON DISTANCE WATER TRAVELED IN 1 MINUTE

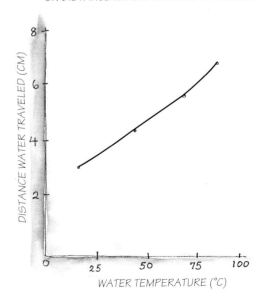

Observations, Ideas, Sketches, Questions

WHAT I WILL TRY	PREDICTED RESULT	ACTUAL RESULT

Hypotheses:

Radiant Color Experiment

Title (decide on this last):

Purpose:

Procedure:

1.

2.

3.

4.

5.

6.

Data: (includes display on separate paper)

Did you hear about the robbery at the laundromat? Two clothespins held up a shirt!

Conclusion:

12. Whack It!

Want to feel amazingly talented? Clear the area for this dramatic demonstration of inertia and gravity.

WARNING: Cardboard will fly at high speeds. The golf ball could possibly be flung as well. Be sure the area is clear of people and breakables.

> **Fear makes the wolf bigger than he is.**
> —*German proverb*

Materials

1 plastic or wooden ruler
1 plastic cup with a smooth rim
Water
1 golf ball
1 Ping-Pong ball, or a small Styrofoam or Nerf ball

The cardboard tube from a roll of paper toweling
1 envelope
1 piece of cardboard or a greeting card that fits snugly into the envelope

1 towel or sponge to wipe splashes
1 egg; optional
One, two, or three additional sets of cardboard tube, cup, and golf ball; optional

I. Whack It!

1. Clear an area of the kitchen counter or a table.
2. Place the cup, two-thirds full of water, close to the edge of the counter near you.
3. Seal the envelope with the cardboard inside and place it flat on top of the cup so that one end of the envelope extends about 3 inches (8 cm) beyond the edge of the counter toward you.
4. The area ahead beyond the cup should be clear of people and breakables because you are about to send the card flying. Hold the bottom end of the ruler firmly in one hand directly below the edge of the card. Pull back on the top end of the ruler with the other hand so that if you were to let go, the flat side of the top end of the ruler would hit the

card sharply. The ruler has become a powerful, spring-loaded whacker. Practice whacking the card several times, resetting the card on the cup after each hit. The card should be hit cleanly and shoot 5–10 feet (2–3 meters) straight ahead. The ruler should not hit the cup.
5. Set the card in its place again. Stand the cardboard tube on the envelope so it is centered above the cup. Look in from each of two sides to be sure the tube is centered.

6. Place the golf ball on the top of the tube. Double check that the tube, ball, and cup are still lined up. Record your prediction of where the ball will land after whacking.
7. Show time! Be sure the area ahead of you is clear. When you are ready, pull the top of the ruler back and let it go!
8. Did the ball land in the cup? If not, practice your whacking technique against a piece of upholstered furniture. Confidence is the key!
9. Record your observations on the record sheet.

II. Whack It!

1. Repeat what you did above except, instead of using a golf ball, substitute a Ping-Pong ball. (If the space in the cardboard tube is too big for the Ping-Pong ball to stand on top, make a seat for the ball using some tape strips.) Record your prediction of where the ball will land.
2. Getting the same result as with the golf ball? Why?
3. Record your observations on the record sheet.

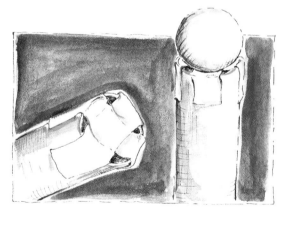

III. Whack It! Exploration

Can you add a second cup/tube/golf ball to your set-up? A third? A fourth? (For three or four, you would need a bigger envelope, maybe 8.5" × 11".) Four at once is quite impressive!

If your whacking skills are well practiced, see if you can get your parents to let you use an egg instead of the golf ball. The egg can be raw or hard boiled depending on your courage. This makes for a dramatic show yet is *almost* fool-proof!

Record your observations.

Vocabulary and concepts appear on page 135.

Observations, Ideas, Sketches, Questions

Your prediction of where golf ball will land: _____

Where golf ball did land: _____

Your prediction of where Ping-Pong ball will land: _____

Where Ping-Pong ball did land: _____

Your hypothesis of why the two balls behave as they do: _____

_____

Results with extra cups/tubes/balls:

Q: What do you get when you drop a grand piano down a mine shaft?
A: You get A flat minor.

Draw a cartoon?:

13. Be a Swinger!

Swinging a cup of water over your head on a tray seems impossible but you can be a pro at it in no time. The laws of physics are in your favor! Your friends will think it's a trick. If your parents ask you what this has to do with science, tell them it relates to planets in their orbits and socks in the washing machine. It does!

WARNING: The tray and cup will be moving at high speeds.
Clear the area of people and breakables.

Materials

1 sturdy serving tray, plastic or metal, any size or shape up to 18 inches (45 cm) across
   (not breakable!)
About 18 feet (6 m) of cord, heavy string, or light rope
Duct tape (most other tapes will not be sticky or strong enough)
1 or more *plastic* cups (transparent plastic cups are nice if you are showing this to others)
Water

I. Be a Swinger!

1. Place the tray upside down on the floor.
2. Cut the cord into two 9-foot (3-m) sections.
3. Lay the pieces of cord in a giant "X" centered
   on the bottom of the tray. The arms of the
   "X" should run past the corners. (If your tray
   is round, ignore any part about corners.)
4. Use duct tape to thoroughly tape the cord to
   the tray bottom. The corners need to be
   taped especially well.
5. Turn the tray over and collect the four
   cord ends in one hand. Make one knot of
   these ends so that the tray will hang level from it. Make several more knots of the four
   cords working closer to the tray. You will hold the knot closest to the tray in your hand
   when you do the swinging. If your cord is slim, tie an old
   sock or rag into that knot so that the rope will be
   easy to grip.
6. Stand with your arms hanging at your sides
   holding the knotted rope in one hand. If the
   tray touches the ground when holding the
   knot closest to the tray, tie another knot lower
   down so that the tray will clear the floor by
   7 or 8 inches (20 cm).
7. In a wide open area outdoors, try swinging
   the tray around from an extended arm. It
   should never hit the ground or anything
   else. Should the tray hit something, the
   cup of water you will be adding to it will
   keep moving until it crashes into
   something. Warn anyone who is
   watching and be sure the area is free
   of breakables. Recheck the duct tape
   often to make sure it is holding well.

8. Put water in the plastic cup and place it in the center of the tray. Now for the fun part!

9. With a straightened arm rotating at the shoulder, swing the tray back and forth in an arc a few times. Then, purposefully, continue the arc into a full circle over your head, high to low. Go around and around. Awesome!

10. Now the challenge is to stop! Do so by changing from full revolutions back to arcs, which then get shorter and shorter. Concentrate! Think about stopping when the tray is just starting down, slowing the swing so the tray won't continue up too high on the other side.

11. Record your observations and questions on the record sheet. How about creating a cartoon of your efforts?

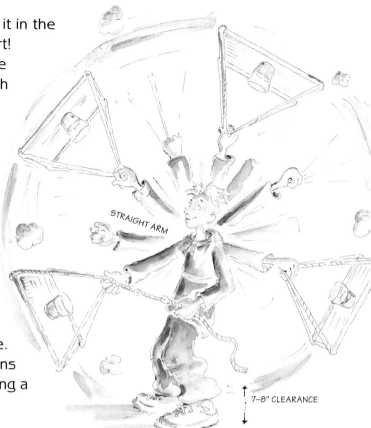

STRAIGHT ARM

7–8" CLEARANCE

II. Swinger Investigations

1. Once you have the swinging technique mastered, think of questions to investigate. Record your predictions before you carry them out.

> Only those who dare to fail greatly can ever achieve greatly.
> —*Robert F. Kennedy*

How fast can you go? Count the number of revolutions the tray makes in 10 seconds with help from someone watching the time. Then calculate the rate of revolutions (revs/minute) by multiplying your count times six. Does the rate of revolutions depend on the amount of water in the cup?

How slowly can you go without the cup falling off?

Can you swing more than one cup? (plastic please!)

Can you stack one cup on top of another with cardboard in between and still do it?

How about making a miniature version of the swinging tray? Your tray could be the size of a computer disc with a plastic vial for the cup or as small as the lid of a film canister with a toothpaste cap for a cup. Do smaller versions work the same way? Are the highest and lowest possible rates of revolutions the same?

2. Record your discoveries.

Vocabulary and concepts appear on page 136.

Observations, Ideas, Sketches, Questions

I. Observations:

Q: What do you give
a seasick elephant?
A: Lots of space!

II. Investigations:

What I Will Try	Predicted Result	Actual Result

Revolution Rate: _____ revolutions/10 seconds × 6 = _____ revolutions/minute
What's the difference between the idea of *rate of revolutions* and *number of revolutions*?

_____

_____

_____

14.
What If Gravity Disappeared?

A Workout for Your Brain

You let go of your dirty socks and they hit the floor. You kick a soccer ball and no matter how hard or high you kick it, a moment later it is back on the ground. Objects have an irresistible attraction to Earth caused by the force called *gravity*. But, what if gravity suddenly disappeared? I assure you that won't happen, but . . . WHAT IF? We are so used to living with the effects of gravity, can you even get your brain to *think* about what would be different if gravity was gone? Well, stretch your brain and give it a try!

Materials

An open mind!

> **He who walks in another's tracks leaves no footprints.**
> —*Joan L. Brannon*

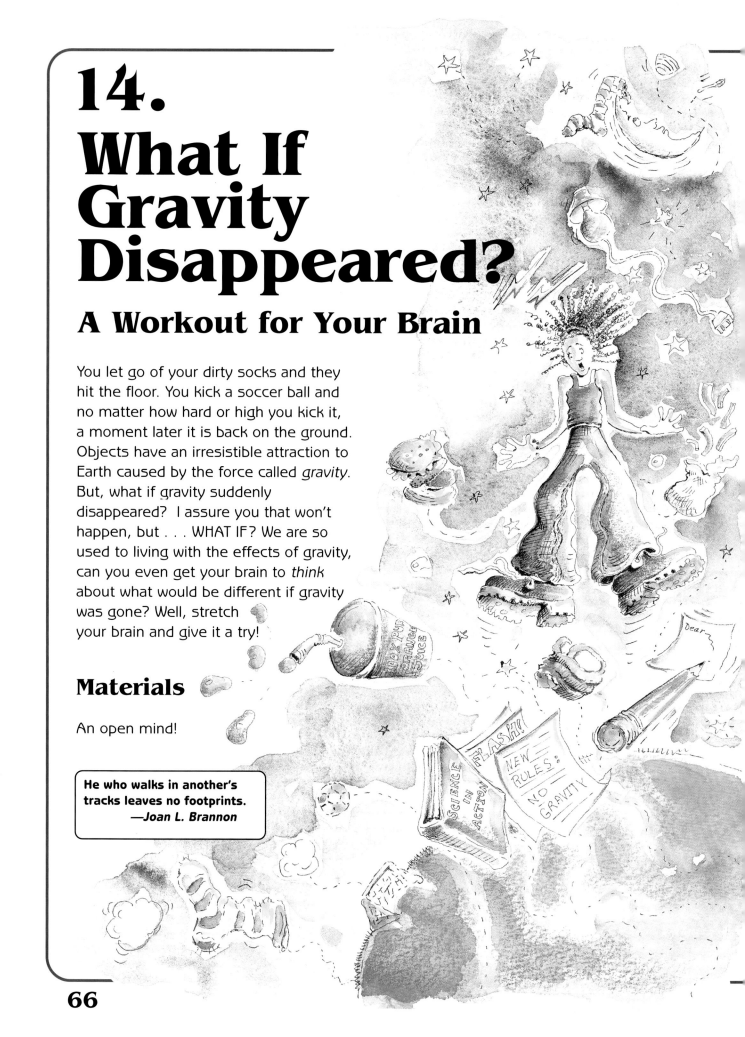

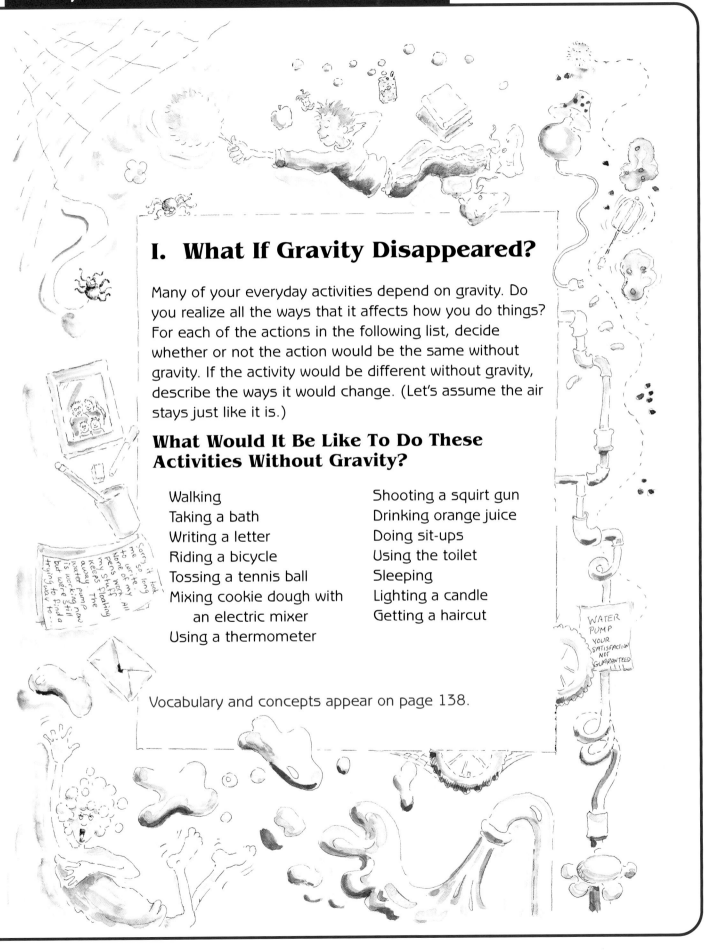

I. What If Gravity Disappeared?

Many of your everyday activities depend on gravity. Do you realize all the ways that it affects how you do things? For each of the actions in the following list, decide whether or not the action would be the same without gravity. If the activity would be different without gravity, describe the ways it would change. (Let's assume the air stays just like it is.)

What Would It Be Like To Do These Activities Without Gravity?

Walking
Taking a bath
Writing a letter
Riding a bicycle
Tossing a tennis ball
Mixing cookie dough with
  an electric mixer
Using a thermometer

Shooting a squirt gun
Drinking orange juice
Doing sit-ups
Using the toilet
Sleeping
Lighting a candle
Getting a haircut

Vocabulary and concepts appear on page 138.

Your Thoughts

ACTION	HOW WOULD THIS ACTION CHANGE IF GRAVITY DISAPPEARED?
Walking	
Taking a bath	
Writing a letter	
Riding a bicycle	
Tossing a tennis ball	
Mixing cookie dough with an electric mixer	
Using a thermometer	
Shooting a squirt gun	
Drinking orange juice	
Doing sit-ups	

ACTION	HOW WOULD THIS ACTION CHANGE IF GRAVITY DISAPPEARED?
Using the toilet	
Sleeping	
Lighting a candle	
Getting a haircut	

II. Gravity Discussions

Now that you have collected your own thoughts on how things would change without gravity, find a parent, neighbor, or friend to talk to and share your thoughts. Does he or she agree with you? Did he or she think of angles you did not think of? Probably you'll end up with some unresolved questions in your mind. Record your questions here.

Questions You Still Have:

Did you hear about the new restaurant on the moon?

The food is good but there's no atmosphere.

15. Where's the Heat?

Perhaps your imagination will be stirred as you puzzle over the flow of heat around a flame and the intriguing motion of a candle burning at both ends.

WARNING: You will be working with a sharp knife and with flames from matches and candles. Keep long hair tied back and clear the area of other flammables.

No one can make you feel inferior without your consent.
—*Eleanor Roosevelt*

Materials

1 candle of any type, upright in a holder.
　Call this *Candle A*.
Wooden kitchen matches
1 plain utility candle or a tapered candle.
　Call this *Candle B*.
1 sheet of aluminum foil, about 18 inches
　(45 cm) long

1 cutting board
1 knife
1 long needle
2 food cans of
　the same height
Pliers or tongs

I. Test the Heat Around a Candle Flame

1. Ask an adult to work with you. Matches and candles are fire hazards.
2. Find a place to work where you can have good ventilation without a direct breeze. Turn on an exhaust fan, open the windows, or go outside to an area blocked from the wind.
3. Light Candle A in its stand.
4. From the side, *slowly* approach the candle at the bottom of the flame with a new, unlit match. See if the match will ignite before it touches the flame.
5. Repeat Step 4, going even more slowly to find the *greatest* distance from the flame that the match head can be and still ignite. Note the distance from the flame by making an actual-size sketch on the record sheet.
6. With a new match, approach the flame again, coming down from above so that the match head is directly above the flame. Go slowly and again note the farthest distance the match head can be from the flame and still ignite.
7. Test all the positions in between in a similar way and record your results by adding to your sketch on the record sheet.
8. What can you conclude about the way heat is distributed around the candle wick?

II. Burn the Candle at Both Ends

1. With adult help, carefully use the knife and cutting board to shape the blunt end of Candle B more like the wick end. In Step 6 that follows, you will be lighting both ends of the candle.

2. Tear off about 18 inches (45 cm) of aluminum foil and put the sheet down to protect the table in your work area from wax and scratches.

3. Find the center of gravity of Candle B by balancing it across a finger. Make a mark on the candle above your finger where it balances.

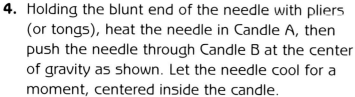

4. Holding the blunt end of the needle with pliers (or tongs), heat the needle in Candle A, then push the needle through Candle B at the center of gravity as shown. Let the needle cool for a moment, centered inside the candle.

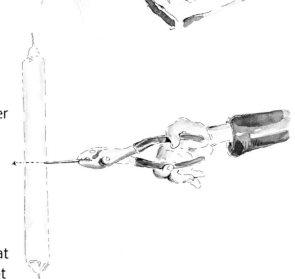

5. Put the two cans on the foil. Set the ends of the needle across the cans so that the candle is free to see-saw. The cans act as a stand. If the candle hangs vertically (up and down), cut a little wax off the low end of the candle so that it balances more side to side. (Perfection is not needed.)

6. Once the candle is balanced, light both ends. Keep flammable materials away from your work area and do not leave burning candles unattended.

7. Watch with patience. For a while, it may seem like nothing much is going to happen, but resist the temptation to mess with your setup! After several minutes the most vigorous action should occur.

8. Record your observations.

Vocabulary and concepts appear on page 141.

Observations, Ideas, Sketches, Questions

**Sketch match locations
around the candle flame:**

Conclusion about heat distribution around wick:

Observations of candle motion:

The human brain is a wonderful thing. It starts working the moment you get up in the morning and doesn't quit until the teacher calls on you.

Hypothesis of why candle moves that way:

16. Whirligig Rocketry

Rocketry principles are illustrated by this simple, but surprising, balloon gadget. Can you predict what the whirligig is going to do?

FLASH

WHOOSH

Materials

1 balloon; about 5 inches (13 cm) in diameter is best, but any size will work

1 bendable drinking straw

Cellophane tape

1 pencil with eraser

1 straight pin

Scissors

A helper during data collection

A stopwatch

> There ain't no cloud so thick that the sun ain't shinin' on t'other side.
> —*Rattlesnake*, an 1870s mountain man

I. Build the Whirligig

1. Stretch the balloon out a few times with your hands, then inflate it (blow it up). This is the only hard part of the whole activity! If you really have trouble, you can fill it once with water from the faucet.

2. Let the air or water out. Your balloon is now stretched and will be easier to inflate later.

3. Trim off the rubber ring at the balloon's opening with scissors.

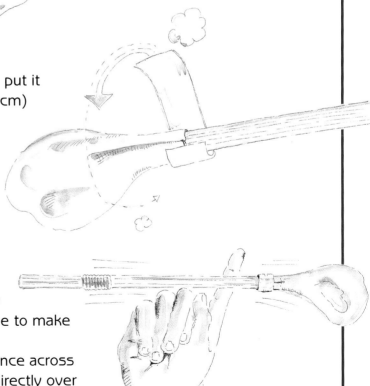

4. Take the long end of the bendable straw and put it into the balloon opening—about 1/2 inch (1 cm) within the balloon.

5. The balloon opening will be too big for the straw, so fold the excess over while stretching the balloon opening slightly for a tight fit. The balloon opening is now adjusted to seal around the straw. Wrap a strip of tape, an inch or two (3–5 cm) long, around the balloon/straw connection so that there are no air leaks.

6. Check the seal by blowing through the straw to inflate the balloon. If it leaks, redo the tape to make an air-tight seal.

7. Find the place on the straw where it will balance across your finger. The straw's center of gravity is directly over your finger where it balances.

8. At the center of gravity, stick the pin all the way through the center of the straw as shown.
9. Push the sharp tip of the pin into your pencil eraser. You are almost ready for action!
10. Bend the straw into a right angle pointed to the side.

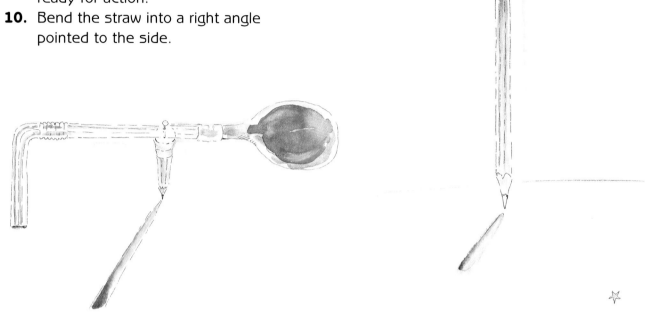

11. Inflate the balloon through the straw and let it go! Neat, huh? Describe your observations on page 78.
12. If you turned the nozzle to the right the first time, turn it to the left now, inflate, and release the balloon again. How does it compare with before? Try different nozzle positions and amounts of air to see what you can learn.

II. What Is the Effect of Nozzle Position on the Number of Spins the Whirligig Makes?

1. Now, seriously experiment with different nozzle (straw opening) positions. The data you collect may or may not match your ideas from your first tries. Try different angles to the side as well as up and down. Sketch the positions you choose at the top of each column of the data table. Inflate the balloon to the same size each time and let it go with the same technique. For each nozzle position you choose, count the total number of spins the whirligig makes for each of three trials (tries). How will you be sure you keep the size of the inflated balloon the same each time? One quick way would be to stand up two thick books facing each other a certain distance apart. Inflate the balloon between them until the sides of the balloon touch both books. Or, inflate the balloon into a small box. Stop inflating when it touches the

sides of the box. Or cut a hole in a sheet of cardboard and inflate the balloon until it fills the hole. Or, think of your own way.

2. It is not easy to count the spins when the balloon is spinning quickly. It will take some practice. You may want to ask someone to help you count.

3. Do three trials with each position. (More would be even better.) Your *average* number of spins for a position will be a more reliable value than any single result.

4. Complete the data table for different nozzle positions. The table shown is one way your data could be organized, but other ways are possible. A good table is well labeled and it is organized so that a reader can understand it quickly.

5. Find the average number of spins for each position you tried and then rank the positions for how well each position moved the balloon. (To get the average, add up all the trial results, then divide by the number of trials you did.)

6. What is the best nozzle position for spinning? State your findings in a sentence under "Conclusion."

7. Should you make a graph? A bar graph would add impact to your data. See the "Graphing Appendix" on page 160 for information on how to set one up.

III. What Is the Effect of the Size of the Nozzle Opening on the Number of Spins *and* on the Rate of Spinning?

1. Using the best nozzle position, repeat three spin trials, but now *time the spinning with a stop watch as well.* You'll need a helper for this. Make predictions before you begin.

2. Keeping the nozzle position the same, reduce the size of the nozzle opening by crimping the end of the straw and wrapping it with a *little* bit of tape. Make your predictions.

3. Once again, count the total number of spins. Complete three trials. Does a narrower opening affect the total number of spins? Does it affect the rate of the spins? *Rate* compares some measured event to how long the event took. The spin rate is the number of spins per second. The word *per* means "for every." It also tells you that a division problem has been done. For example, if you travel 100 miles in 2 hours, your rate of travel is 100 miles ÷ 2 hours, or 50 miles *per* hour.

4. Reduce the size of the nozzle opening once more by retaping it with a deeper crimp. Collect your data and complete your calculations.

5. State your findings in a sentence under "Conclusion."

6. Should you make a graph? A bar graph (or, if you measure the nozzle opening, a line graph) would add impact to this data as well. See the "Graphing Appendix" on page 160 for information on graphing your results.

Vocabulary and concepts appear on page 143.

Observations, Ideas, Sketches, Questions

I. Observations

II. Nozzle Position Experiment
Size of balloon kept the same for each trial by:

DATA FOR DIFFERENT NOZZLE POSITIONS:

	NUMBER OF SPINS			
Position Sketch:				
Prediction:				
Trial 1:				
Trial 2:				
Trial 3:				
Sum of Trials:				
Average:				
Rank: 1= Most Spins				

Conclusion:

Hypothesize:
What do you think is going on? Why are some positions better than others?

III. Nozzle Size Experiment

DATA FOR DIFFERENT NOZZLE OPENINGS:

Position Sketch:	REGULAR NOZZLE		NARROWER NOZZLE		NARROWEST NOZZLE	
	# Spins	Time (seconds)	# Spins	Time (seconds)	# Spins	Time (seconds)
Prediction:						
Trial 1:						
Trial 2						
Trial 3:						
Sum of Trials:						
Average:						
Average Rate:						

Conclusion:

Hypothesize:
What do you think is going on? Why are some nozzle sizes better than others?

Danny Driver: Please look outside...is my blinker on?
Peggy Passenger: Yes. No. Yes. No. Yes. No. Yes.

17.
Pop
Can
Pedestal

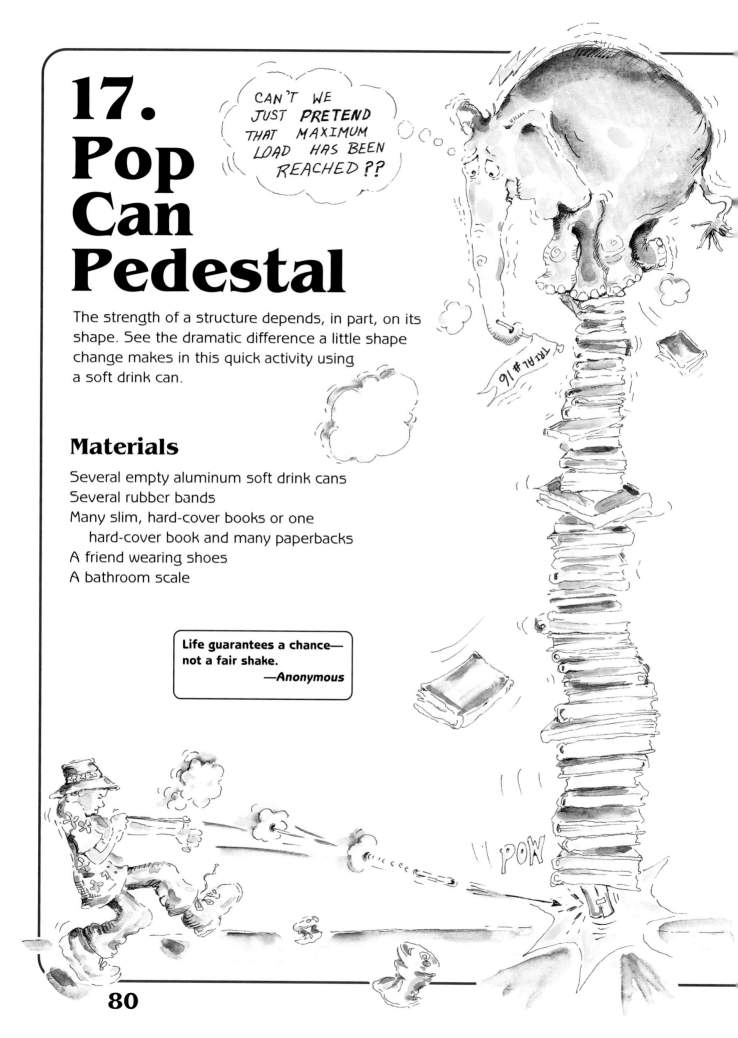

CAN'T WE JUST **PRETEND** THAT MAXIMUM LOAD HAS BEEN REACHED ??

The strength of a structure depends, in part, on its shape. See the dramatic difference a little shape change makes in this quick activity using a soft drink can.

Materials

Several empty aluminum soft drink cans
Several rubber bands
Many slim, hard-cover books or one
    hard-cover book and many paperbacks
A friend wearing shoes
A bathroom scale

> **Life guarantees a chance—
> not a fair shake.**
> —*Anonymous*

I. Pop Can Pedestal

1. Have your friend gently step up onto an empty soda pop can with one foot centered on the top of the can. The friend should hold on to a chair for security. Explain that the can could collapse at any time.
2. Sit or lie down 3 feet (1 m) away from the can and shoot the can with a rubber band. If nothing happens, try again.

II. Pop Can Pedestal Investigation

Can you find out the weight limit for an undented can? You could have a heavier person stand on the can. Or you could put a pack and/or shopping bags on the person and gradually load him or her with heavy objects. Make a plan and carry it out. Record your steps and your results. Realize that when the can collapses, the maximum load has just been *passed*. When you know the approximate weight that will crush the can, you can try again with smaller weight additions to get closer to the actual maximum. The more trials you do, the better your value for the maximum load.

III. Paper Pedestal Investigation

How much weight do you think a paper tube of the same diameter as the soft drink can could hold? Take a new sheet of copy paper, wrap it around a soft drink can to make a tube, and tape the free end.

Remove the can. Gather a stack of slim hardcover books or paperback books and feel the weight of a few. Predict the number of books the tube will hold, then do a test. Carefully place a hardcover book on top of the tube, then add one book at a time on top of that one to reach the maximum load. Make sure the books are centered over the tube. Find the weight of the books the tube supported on your bathroom scale. Do three trials and average the results.

- Is the maximum load different if you leave the can inside the paper tube?
- If you double the amount of paper, is the maximum load doubled?

If you find that the strength of the paper is proportional to the number of sheets, you can calculate the number of sheets of paper needed to support your weight. Then you can test your calculation by making the tube of that many sheets and standing on it.

What happens if the tube is shot with a rubber band?

Vocabulary and concepts appear on page 144.

Observations, Ideas, Sketches, Questions

SOFT DRINK CAN MAXIMUM LOAD (POUNDS OR KILOGRAMS)

Estimate:	
Trial 1	
Trial 2	
Trial 3	
Average	

PAPER TUBE MAXIMUM LOAD

	SINGLE SHEET TUBE		PAPER TUBE WITH CAN		TWO SHEET TUBE	
	BOOKS	LBS/KG	BOOKS	LBS/KG	BOOKS	LBS/KG
Estimates:						
Trial 1						
Trial 2						
Trial 3						
Average						

Minimum Number of Paper Sheets Needed to Hold Me:

Your weight: _____ ÷ Weight held by one sheet: _____ = Number of sheets: _____

Q: What did the hat say to the hatrack?
A: You stay here while I go on a head.

18. Ramp

The challenge here is to build a structure that will allow a Ping-Pong ball to roll from top to bottom *at the slowest possible rate* without stopping.

Materials

1 Ping-Pong ball
25 pieces of copy paper (from the recycle bin, if possible!)
1 standard-size 22" × 28" (56 × 71 cm) piece of poster board; foam core board is helpful, but not essential

Cellophane tape, any amount up to one roll
Scissors
1 stopwatch
1 partner, optional

> Think you can, think you can't; either way, you'll be right.
> —*Henry Ford*

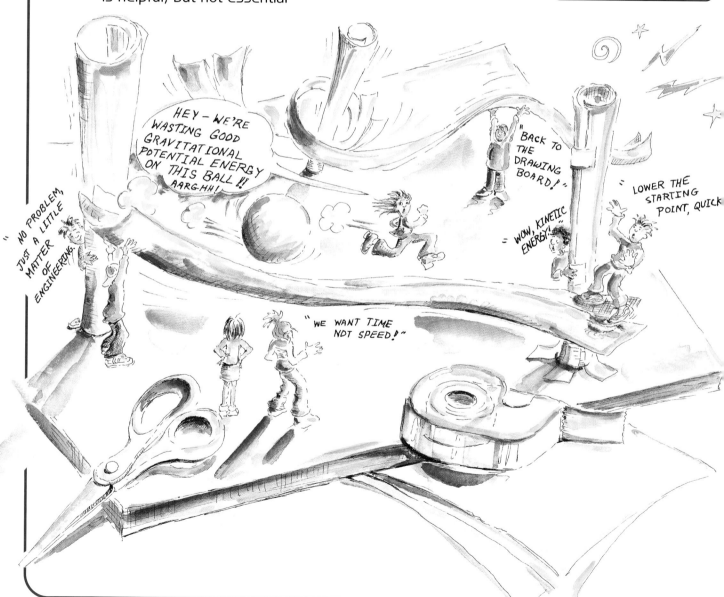

84

Rules

1. Use just the materials specified.
2. The poster board's function is to serve as a base. The paper structure may attach to the base but may not touch any other object. (The board allows you to move your work and keep it all in one piece. If your structure were taped to the kitchen table, that could be a problem at dinner time.)
3. The ramp is to be built in 90 minutes or less.
4. The ramp is evaluated by ball-rolling time. The time starts when the ball is placed on the structure and stops when either the ball stops or the ball reaches the level of the poster board, whichever comes first.

Principles to Consider

REALLY!
GET A HOLD ON YOURSELF!
YOU'VE GOT TO WORK ON
THE ANGLES. D'YA THINK
SLOWNESS HAPPENS
OVERNIGHT??

*   The source of energy for the rolling of the ball comes from gravity (gravitational potential energy). The greater the total height of the ramp, the more energy available for rolling the ball.
*   The more gentle the slope of the ramp, the more slowly the ball will roll.
*   Tubes and certain folds can make paper more rigid for supporting structures.
*   With the limited supply of paper, you will want to use the minimum that will do the job at every step along the way.

GOTTA WORK ON
THE VERTICAL SUPPORTS...
NO COLLAPSING OR
BENDING, O.K.?

*   You will have the best results if you design your structure so that it would stand even if it wasn't taped down.

Begin

1. Design your ramp using sketches.
2. Count 25 sheets of paper.
3. Go to work!
4. When you are finished, do three runs and average the longest two times for an official time for your structure.
5. Record your insights.
6. Try again and see if you can increase your time with engineering improvements.

Vocabulary and concepts appear on page 145.

Observations, Ideas, Sketches, Questions

Ramp Plans:

Actual Ramp Sketches and Times:

Q: What do you call a rabbit who swims with sharks?
A: Dinner!

Things That Worked Well:

Things That Did Not Work Well:

19. Tall Tower

Your challenge is to build the tallest possible freestanding tower from a single piece of paper and 1 foot (30 cm) of tape.

Imagination is more important than knowledge.
—Albert Einstein

Materials

1 sheet of copy
 paper
12 inches (30 cm)
 of cellophane tape
Scissors

Rules

1. Use only the materials specified.
2. "Freestanding" means not stuck into or onto anything. You should be able to
   pick the tower up and set it down somewhere else. Put it on a table or on smooth
   flooring.
3. The tower is to be built in one hour or less.
4. The completed tower must remain standing for at least 30 seconds.

Construction Principles to Think About

- Tubes and folds can make paper more rigid, able to support more weight.
- Balance is critical. For an object to stand at all, the center of its weight must be
  directly above its base. To stand with stability, the center of its weight should be low
  and centered above the base.
- With such a limited supply of paper and tape, you will want to use the smallest
  amounts that will do the job at every step along the way.
- The bottom of the tower is the base for both balance and strength. It must hold the
  weight of all the rest.

Begin

1. Design your tower by sketching it.
2. Measure and cut the correct length of tape.
3. Go to work!
4. Record your observations. Sketch and measure the completed tower. It will be easier to
   measure lying down (not you, the tower!) after it is done.
5. Try again, and see if you can build a taller tower with engineering improvements.

Vocabulary and concepts appear on page 146.

Observation, Ideas, Sketches, Questions

Tower Plans:

> Did you hear about the butcher who backed into the meat grinder and got a little behind in his work?

Completed Tower Sketches and Heights:

Things That Worked Well:

Things That Didn't Work Well:

20. Portable Alarm

Want to be alerted when someone enters the room? Build an alarm with a special switch triggered by opening the door. No electrical experience necessary!

Materials

1 empty cereal or snack cracker box
1 fresh 9-volt radio battery
1 buzzer from an electronic store, 6–9 volts
1 narrow, clean, plastic prescription pill
    container from the pharmacy

2 marbles, steel or glass
Aluminum foil
Cellophane tape, 1/2 inch wide
Pen or pencil

The Big Picture

The alarm is built into the cracker or cereal box. When the box is standing up, the buzzer is off. When the box is tipped over, the buzzer turns on automatically. Let's say your bedroom door opens *in* to your room. To set the alarm, you stand it up just inside the door. When the door is opened, the box falls over and . . . BUZZ! You can take it to any room.

Inside the box, three items—the buzzer, the battery, and a switch—will be connected with homemade aluminum wires. For the buzzer to work, electricity from the battery must be able to travel in a continuous path or circuit through the parts. The job of the switch, which you will make, is to continue the path sometimes, and at other times to break the path so that the electricity cannot flow. This switch works by the use of a marble covered with foil. When the marble rolls into place, it connects two wires to complete the circuit. BUZZ. When it rolls back to its first position, the path is broken. No buzz.

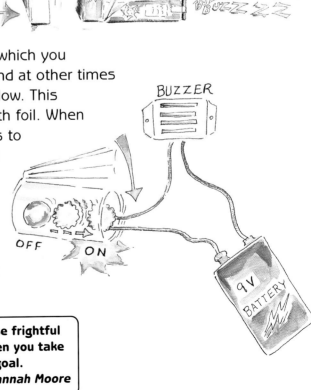

All parts of this alarm are safe to handle, assuming your battery is new and not leaking. If you ever see a battery that is *leaking*, dispose of it at once without directly touching it (battery acid is caustic).

> **Obstacles are those frightful things you see when you take your eyes off the goal.**
> **—Hannah Moore**

I. Build the Alarm

1. Make sure the buzzer works by firmly touching each of its two bare wire tips to different terminals at the top of the battery.

2. Make three lengths of aluminum foil wire: 2 inches (5 cm), 5 inches (13 cm), and 8 inches (20 cm), as follows:

   a. Tear off a strip of aluminum foil 2 inches (5 cm) wide.

   b. Cut the strip to the right length.

   c. Tear off a piece of tape 2 inches (5 cm) longer than the foil and lay it flat, sticky side down, centered on the foil 1/2 inch (1 cm) in from one edge. One inch (2.5 cm) of tape extends past each foil end.

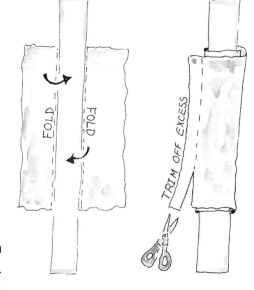

   d. Fold the narrow edge of foil over the back of the tape, then fold the other side over and trim off the excess foil. Your wire is a ribbon of three layers of foil around a piece of tape. The foil will carry electricity. The tape at the ends is for sticking the wire in place.

3. Wire the battery as follows:

   a. Attach the 2-inch (5-cm) wire to one of the battery terminals by taping as shown, scrunching the foil around the terminal post, then taping around the battery.

   b. Attach the 8-inch (20-cm) wire in a similar way to the other terminal but have it come in from the opposite side. Tape all around. These two pieces of foil must NOT directly touch each other for any length of time. If they do, the battery will quickly burn out.

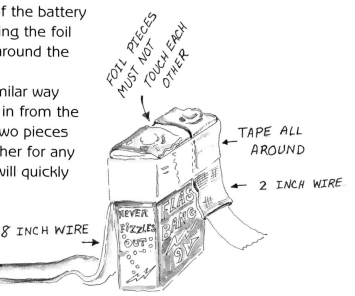

   c. Test the connections you just made by firmly touching the bare tips of the buzzer wires to the foil wires, one buzzer wire to each foil wire. If the buzzer doesn't work, you will have to redo the connections. They must be secure.

4. Make and connect the switch as follows:

a. Attach the 5-inch (13-cm) wire inside the pill container so that about 3/4 inch (2 cm) of foil is in the container. About 1/2 inch (1 cm) beyond the rim of the container, fold this wire over on itself and against the outside of the container. Wrap around it with tape.

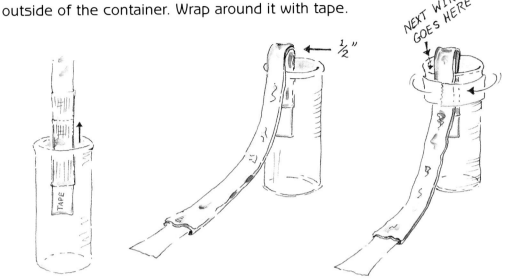

b. Attach the free end of the 8-inch (20-cm) wire right next to the left side of the one you just placed, close to, but not touching, it. Fold the wire as you did for the other one and tape it all around the container.

c. Place one marble in the container. Wrap a second marble with foil and then press it firmly against a table top to flatten any bumps. When the foil-covered marble is round, place it in the container as well. There should be a gap above the marbles before the metal of the wires begins.

d. Attach a 2-inch (5-cm) length of tape to the outside of the foil tabs sticking up out of the container. The tabs should be close to each other on the tape but not touching. Apply the sticky side of a *very* skinny strip of tape to the sticky gap between the tabs so that when the tabs are folded down to be a partial cover of the container, there is no sticky spot. Fold the tabs down and attach the tape down the sides of the container.

5. Add the buzzer as follows:

   a. Lay the bare wire tip of one of the buzzer wires across the foil near the free end of the 2-inch (5-cm) wire so that you can fold the sticky side of the tape down to hold it in place.

   b. Attach the other buzzer wire to the free end of the 5-inch (13-cm) wire the same way.

6. Test the circuit by turning the container over part way so that the foil-covered marble rolls to the top and makes a connection between the two foil tabs. The buzzer should sound. If the buzzer does not turn on, you need to track down the cause of the problem. Probably, there is a bad connection. Possibly, the battery burned out or the buzzer is faulty. How can you test the possibilities?

7. Mount your circuit into the cardboard box as follows:

   a. Use scissors to cut the front of the box at the left side and across the bottom so that the front of the box can open like a door.

   b. Rest the box on its back with the front open.

   c. Set the alarm parts into the box a little above the middle of the box.

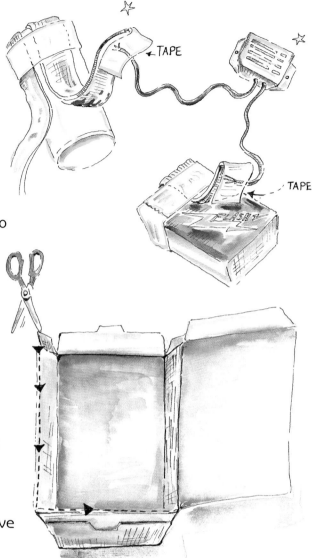

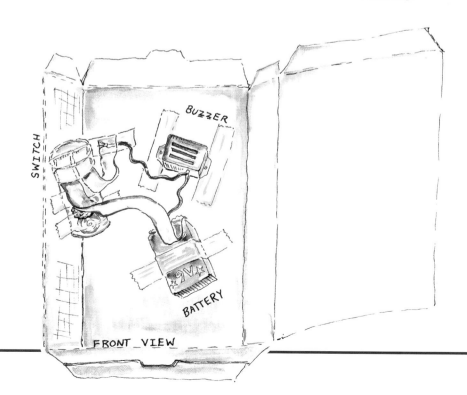

FRONT VIEW

d. The switch (pill container) needs to be positioned carefully, so attach it first. Tape it to the *left* side of the box about halfway up, tilted forward as much as it can be without sticking out beyond the edge of the box. The two wires coming out of the container face you. Tape the container firmly into place, keeping the wires free.

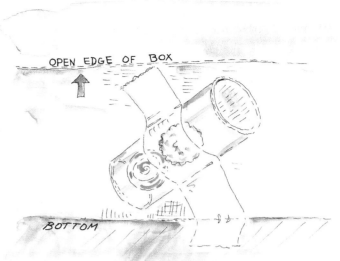

e. Tape the battery flat to the back of the box in the center.

f. Tape the buzzer to the back of the box above the battery.

8. Close the box, hold it upright, then tilt it toward you. The buzzer should turn on as the ball rolls into place to complete the circuit. If this does not happen, you need to trouble-shoot. Is the ball rolling? Are the tabs of the container in the right position?

9. If it's working, tape the box closed and tape a capped pen on the top so that it extends (reaches out) beyond the back.

10. Place the box on your side of a closed door. Open the door in to you so that it knocks the box over. Voilà!

II. Going Further

Can you improve on this design?

Can you insulate your wires?

What about making a second switch so that you could have your alarm either "off" (no matter what position it is in) or "ready"?

Can you invent other uses for the buzzer, such as a part of a game or a clubhouse doorbell?

Vocabulary and concepts appear on page 147.

Observations, Ideas, Sketches, Questions

Atom: "Oh, no! I lost an electron!"
Atom's friend: "Are you sure? How do you know?"
Atom: "I'm positive!"

21. Bubble Extravaganza

There are a zillion fun things to do with bubbles. This section will get you started with a reliable recipe and ideas for hours of play . . . uh, I mean serious scientific investigation. Be sure to clean up well afterward. Keep the management happy!

Materials

Ultra Joy, Ultra Ivory, or Ultra Dawn dishwashing soap (other brands may not work as well)

Glycerin, optional; found at the pharmacy; ask for a 12-oz. (350-mL) bottle if you plan to make bubble solution often

Several drinking straws

Covered storage container(s)

Plastic 1 gallon (4 L) milk jug(s)

Soup can with top and bottom removed

Objects from around the house to try as bubble wands

Pizza pan, cookie pan, or serving tray

String

Wire; 16–18 gauge steel is about the right stiffness. Or use what you have handy, such as coat hangers.

Pliers for shaping wire wands

Thread

Hula-hoop and small kid's swimming pool, optional

I. Make the Solution

Read ahead to see what projects you want to do so you can decide how much solution to make.

> Words are mere bubbles of water, but deeds are drops of gold.
> —*Chinese proverb*

For nearly two cups of solution:

1. Choose a container with a lid.
2. Combine 5 tablespoons (75 mL) dishwashing liquid, 1 tablespoon (15 mL) glycerin, and $1^1/_2$ cups (360 mL) water in your container. The proportions are about 1:1/5:5.
3. Stir mixture *gently* and it is ready!

For almost one gallon of solution:

1. Thoroughly wash out a plastic milk jug.
2. Combine $2^1/_2$ cups (575 mL) of dishwashing liquid, $^1/_2$ cup (115 mL) glycerin, and $12^1/_2$ cups (3 L) of water in the jug.
3. Stir mixture *gently* and it is ready!

For small projects, working in the kitchen near the sink is best. For big, messy ones, work outdoors or in a garage. A cloudy day with no wind is definitely the best weather for lasting bubbles outdoors.

II. Investigate Bubble-Making Tools

Try making bubbles with different items from around the house. Choose objects with openings to hold a film of bubble solution. Make sure you have permission to use them! Now, see if you can make bubbles with them. Dip them into the solution. For some of the larger items, you may want to pour the solution into a large bowl for dipping.

Metal egg dipper from last year's Easter eggs?
Kitchen utensils such as a slotted spoon?
The handle of a coffee mug?
A Lego creation?
A paper clip?
A cardboard toilet paper roll?
Plastic bath toys?
String?

Which method of bubble-making works better, blowing or waving the tool? What is the most surprising bubble-making object you found? Record your observations.

III. Design Your Own Bubble Wands

Use the wire and, if necessary, a pair of pliers, to make different shapes and sizes of bubble wands.

Can you make different *shapes* of bubbles with the wands?
What style wand do you like the best?
Are you making a mess yet?
Record your observations on page 103.

IV. Investigate Bubbles on a Tray

Pour some solution onto a pizza pan or cookie tray and use the straw or the soup can to blow bubbles there.

How big a bubble you can create?
How tiny a bubble can you make?
Can you make rows of bubbles all the same size?
How do bubbles join and connect?
Can you blow a bubble inside another bubble? How many nested bubbles
   (not touching one another) can you create?
Can you make a bubble that floats around inside a bubble dome?
Can you put a finger through a bubble? A hand? Your whole arm? Does the skin
   need to be wet?
Record your discoveries. Diagrams are a good way to do this.

V. Human Bubble Wand

Do this over the sink if you are indoors. Dip your hand into the solution to pick up a soap film in the circle of an O.K. sign. Blow. Dip two hands forming an "O" to pick up a soap film between them in the circle above the thumbs. Blow.

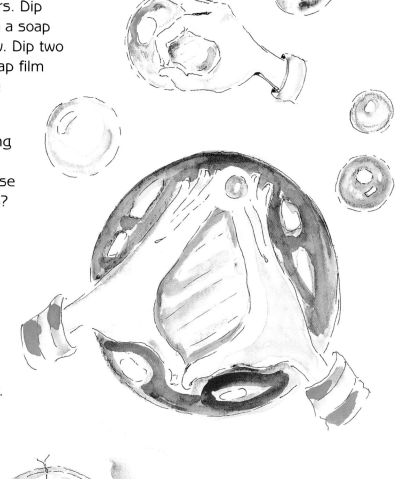

- What happens if you quit blowing before the bubble is formed?
- Are there other ways you can use just your body to make bubbles?
- Record your observations.

VI. A Perfect Circle

1. Make a wand out of wire as shown.
2. Cut a 10-inch (25-cm) length of thread. At one end, tie a loop about 1 inch (2.5 cm) in diameter.
3. At the other end, tie the thread onto the side of the wand and dip the wand with thread into your solution.
4. Remove the wand and hold it to the side so that the thread loop is surrounded by soap film. Use a dry toothpick or pencil tip to break the soap film inside the loop. Neat?

- Does string work as well as thread?
- What kind of bubble do you get from the wand now?
- Record your observations.

VII. Bubble Trampoline

Usually, touching a bubble with a dry object causes it to burst. Bubbles will, however, bounce off fuzzy fabrics such as fleece and wool. Try catching a bubble wearing wool or fleece gloves. You and a partner can make a bubble trampoline out of a wool sweater by holding it taut from four corners. Can you get the bubbles to bounce? Try blowing a few bubbles over carpeting. (Ask your parents first, or use a carpet remnant.)

- What worked the best?
- Record your observations.

VIII. Kid in a Tube

This variation is great fun for a group of people to enjoy. Swimming suits or old clothes should be worn. You need:

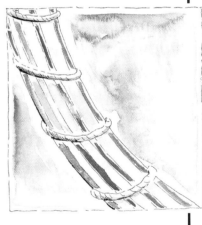

A toddler's plastic swimming pool
A hula-hoop that fits in the bottom of the pool
2–3 gallons (8–11 L) of soap solution
A ball of cotton string
A stepstool or a pair of bricks to stand on in the pool

Wind the string around and around the tubing of the hula-hoop and tie the ends when they meet after winding around the circle. This will help the hoop to pick up enough bubble solution for extra big bubbles.

Make 2–3 gallons (8–11 L) of bubble solution in pitchers or clean gallon milk jugs. Start with 2 gallons (8 L) and see if that is enough to cover the bottom of the pool. Make the third if you need to.

Place the stepstool in the pool. Pour in the soap solution around it. Swoosh the hula-hoop in the solution to cover it well. Have a friend stand on the stool. Lift the hula-hoop with two wetted hands, pulling up a giant bubble tube. If you are tall enough, you may be able to twist the hoop to the side above your friend to finish off the end of the bubble.

- What else can you do with this giant bubble maker?
- Record your observations.

IX. Crystal Bubbles

Outdoors

You will be able to do this outdoors if you live somewhere that gets below freezing in the winter.

1. When it is well *below* freezing outside (maybe 15° F or less; –9°C or less), use any simple bubble wand to blow bubbles outside. Watch!

2. Catch a bubble on your wand and watch it.

Indoors

Sometimes, it is possible to get a captured bubble to freeze in a freezer.

1. Stick the handle end of a bubble wand into a lump of clay or a bagel or something that will allow it to stand.

2. Blow some bubbles in the kitchen.

3. Catch one or more on your wand.

4. Set the bubble stand with bubble into the freezer quickly. Close the freezer door gently. Wait 5 minutes, then check it.

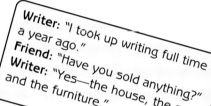

Writer: "I took up writing full time a year ago."
Friend: "Have you sold anything?"
Writer: "Yes—the house, the car, and the furniture."

X. Make Your Own Gifts

How about giving homemade bubble solution and a wire wand for a holiday present? Glue a snazzy personalized label onto a recycled bottle filled with solution, tie a ribbon on the wand, and, PRESTO, you have a unique gift!

Vocabulary and concepts appear on page 148.

Observations, Ideas, Sketches, Questions

Bubble Tools and Wands:

Trampoline:

Bubbles on a Tray:

Kid in a Tube:

Human Bubble Wand:

Crystal Bubbles:

A Perfect Circle:

What Else?

22. Delicious Ice Cream . . . Yum!

Isn't it strange that salt is used to *melt* ice on the roads, yet it is the essential ingredient in making ice cream *freeze*? It's true! Make your own ice cream, then dig into the science behind *change of state*, *freezing point depression*, and *conduction*.

Materials

1/2 cup (120 mL) half and half cream/milk product

1 tablespoon (15 mL) sugar

1/8 teaspoon (0.5 mL) vanilla extract or flavoring

1 empty, clean metal food can such as a soup can

1 popsicle stick, a small wooden spoon, or a sturdy plastic spoon

1 small piece of aluminum foil to cover the can

A 5-quart or 10-inch diameter (5-L or 25-cm diameter) plastic, not metal, bucket or food storage container

Enough crushed or small-cubed ice to nearly fill the bucket

2 cups salt

Thermometer, optional

The Big Picture

The first three items on the materials list are the ice cream ingredients. They will go into the washed metal can, which is the ice cream freezer. The salt and the ice will go into the bucket in alternating layers built up around the metal can. You don't want to get any of the ice or salt in your ice cream. That would *not* be tasty. The salt and ice together make the can cold enough for the ice cream to freeze.

CREAM
SUGAR VANILLA

ICE & SALT LAYERS

Ice Cream Procedure

1. Measure the cream, sugar, and vanilla as you add them to the metal can, then stir. Don't increase the amounts or you will have to wait too long for the ice cream to freeze.
2. Place the can in the refrigerator while you start to prepare its nest of salty ice.
3. Put a layer of ice about 1 inch (2–3 cm) deep into the empty bucket.
4. Generously pour salt all over the ice.
5. Add another layer of ice and again pour salt over it.
6. Take the can out of the refrigerator and cover the top with a small piece of foil. The use of foil is to make sure that salt doesn't get into the can and to help keep out heat.

7. Put the can in the center of the bucket on top of the salt/ice layers.

8. Continue building up alternating layers of salt and ice around the can until the salt and ice reach almost to the top. The layers should be tightly packed.

9. Remove the foil lid so you can use your stick or spoon to stir the cream mixture well.

10. Start recording your observations on the record sheet. Start with time zero, and note the actual clock time.

11. Let the can sit in its nest, re-covered with foil, for 5 minutes. After the 5-minute wait, remove the foil and check for signs of freezing by using your stick or spoon to thoroughly scrape the insides of the can. If you can't feel or see any solids, let the can sit longer, checking every 2 minutes. While you are waiting, record what is going on every 5 minutes. Try not to warm the can by handling it any more than is necessary.

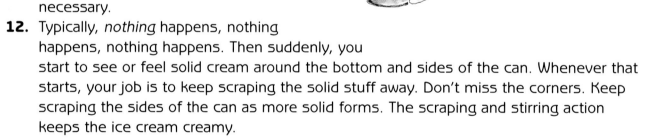

12. Typically, *nothing* happens, nothing happens, nothing happens. Then suddenly, you start to see or feel solid cream around the bottom and sides of the can. Whenever that starts, your job is to keep scraping the solid stuff away. Don't miss the corners. Keep scraping the sides of the can as more solid forms. The scraping and stirring action keeps the ice cream creamy.

13. You can eat your ice cream at any point. If you can stand to wait long enough, it will get quite hard, but it tastes great when it reaches the thickness of a milk shake, too. Once the ice cream is as firm as you want it to be, you can add a topping such as chocolate sauce, whipped cream, or candy pieces. Mmmm! Your ice/salt nest will work for several batches if one serving isn't enough for you.

14. If you have a weather or multipurpose thermometer, use it to find the temperature of the salt/ice/water mixture in the bucket. Compare it with the temperature of plain ice water. Record.

Vocabulary and concepts appear on page 150.

Observations, Ideas, Sketches, Questions

Time Elapsed	Clock Time	Observations
0 minutes	_____	_____
		_____
5 minutes	_____	_____
		_____
10 minutes	_____	_____
		_____
15 minutes	_____	_____
		_____
20 minutes	_____	_____
		_____
25 minutes	_____	_____
		_____
30 minutes	_____	_____
		_____
35 minutes	_____	_____
		_____
40 minutes	_____	_____

Temperature of Salt/Ice Water: _____

Temperature of Plain Ice Water: _____

Bob: "I just got an ice cream cone for my brother."
Bill: "Good swap!"

23. Meringue Dessert Cups

This meringue will take a bit longer than the instant one you may have made earlier but it is *delicious*. Did you know that a chef is a kind of chemist? Fill these cups with ice cream or fruit and whipped cream for a gourmet delight!

Materials

2 small bowls
Mixing bowl
Electric mixer
2 cookie sheets
1 brown grocery bag
   or wax paper

3 eggs at room
   temperature
1 teaspoon (5 mL)
   vanilla
1/4 teaspoon (1 mL)
   cream of tartar

1 cup (230 mL)
   sugar
A dash of salt
1 air-tight storage
   container

> **Kindness gives birth to kindness.**
> **—Sophocles**

I. Make the Meringue

1. Preheat the oven to 250° F.
2. To separate the white from the yolk, crack an egg in half and hold it upright over a bowl while you lift off the top half of the shell. As you remove the top, some of the egg white will slide into the bowl while the yolk stays in the bottom shell. Pour the unbroken yolk from shell to shell to get the rest of the egg white to dribble out into the bowl. Put the yolk into a second bowl to save for another use. If the egg separation is successful, move the white to the mixing bowl and go on to do the next egg the same way. You don't want to get any yolk in the white, so start over with a new egg and a clean bowl if you break a yolk. Scramble your mistakes for breakfast.

   egg white only

3. Add the vanilla, cream of tartar, and a dash of salt.
4. Mix on high speed (whip) until you can make soft peaks of white that will stay in place.
5. Continue whipping while gradually sprinkling in sugar, a tablespoon at a time. All the sugar needs to be well dissolved.
6. You are finished whipping when the meringue is glossy and does not feel gritty on your tongue. The meringue forms stiff peaks when you lift the beaters.

Nice Stiff Peaks!

7. Cut pieces of the clean grocery bag to fit the cookie sheets.

8. Spoon the meringue onto the paper-lined sheets in 10–12 mounds. Twirl the spoon backward to put a cup-shaped depression in the center of each mound.

9. Bake at 250° F for 1 hour. Then turn off the oven but leave the meringues inside to dry for another 2 hours. It is OK to let them stay in the oven overnight.

10. Store the meringue dessert cups in an air-tight container.

11. To eat, fill the meringue with goodies of your choice:

    Fresh fruit and whipped cream?
    Ice cream and fudge sauce?
    Pudding?
    Enjoy!

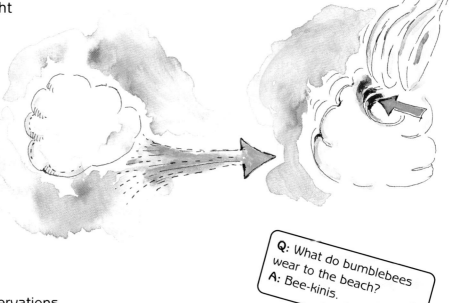

Q: What do bumblebees wear to the beach?
A: Bee-kinis.

12. Record your observations.

II. Meringue Investigation

To conserve time and materials, split batches into two or more parts and try variations on one portion. Careful measuring and comparison to standard-recipe meringues is needed for reliable conclusions.

> What happens if you leave a meringue dessert cup out uncovered for several days?
> What if you omit the cream of tartar?
> What if you get some yolk mixed in with the white?
> What if you use powdered (confectioners') sugar instead of granulated sugar?
> What if . . .
> What if . . . Write *your* questions.

Record your observations.

Vocabulary and concepts appear on page 152.

Observations, Ideas, Sketches, Questions

Regular Meringue Cups:

Results of Investigations:

24. Fabulous Play Gloop

Give yourself plenty of time for Gloop play because once you get your hands on this stuff you won't want to quit. Make long snakes and thin sheets, blow bubbles, have funnel races. You are limited only by your imagination.

> **Honesty is the first chapter of the book of wisdom.**
> —*Thomas Jefferson*

Materials

Elmer's Glue-All (some other brands don't work)
Sta-Flo Liquid Starch (some other brands don't work)
Food coloring (optional)
1 cereal bowl
1 spoon

1 drinking straw
1 large balloon, not inflated
Funnels (can be made with adult help by cutting the top third from a plastic 2-liter bottle. Make a cut with a utility blade, then continue with scissors.)
1 zip top bag, 1 quart (1 liter) size

I. Making the Gloop

1. Clear a space on the kitchen countertop. Don't try to work over paper.
2. Roll up your sleeves. If white glue dries on your clothes, it won't wash out.
3. Measure 1 tablespoon (14 mL) of white glue into the bowl. Stir into it 4 or 5 drops of food coloring, if you like.
4. Add $1\frac{1}{2}$ tablespoons (21 mL) liquid starch gradually to the glue, stirring vigorously as you go.
5. Once you have stirred the two together as well as you can with the spoon, pour a little more liquid starch onto the palms of your hands and pick up the messy glob. Blend the Gloop further by squeezing and folding it with your hands.
6. At first, the Gloop may stick to your skin, but as you work it, it will get less sticky and start to gather up stray bits from your skin and the counter.
7. The mixture should become well blended, soft and pliable, and it should not stick to your skin. If it is still sticky, put some additional starch on your hands and work it in. If it separates into many rubbery blobs that don't unite, try to work in additional glue. (It is easier to add starch than to add glue.) If you haven't added coloring, the Gloop will be a very pale blue due to the color of the starch.

1 tablespoon glue

$1\frac{1}{2}$ tablespoons starch

8. You can still add food color at this point if you don't mind getting colorful hands from working it in. In fact, you could separate the Gloop into parts and add a different color to each part.

9. You can make as big a batch as you like once you know the texture you are aiming for. Start off with a ratio of 2 parts glue to 3 parts starch. Adjust proportions as needed until your Gloop is the right consistency.

II. Messing Around

1. What are you doing still looking at the book? Dig in! Play around! Go to town!

Does it bounce?
Does it tear?
Can you make thin sheets?
Will it hold water?
Can you braid it?
What is the longest
   continuous strand you can make?
Can you makes noise with it?
Can you blow bubbles with it? (Bubbles
   are easy to make using the straw.
   Wrap a wad of Gloop around the straw
   and blow gently. Or, insert the end of the
   straw under a blob of it on the counter and blow.
   Can you make a bubble bigger than your head?)
What if you freeze it?
Will it stream through a funnel?
What kind of artistic creation can you make with Gloop?

Q: What happened to the cat who swallowed a ball of wool?
A: She had mittens!

2. You can make stress balls by filling 9- or 11-inch (23 to 28 cm) balloons (the bigger, the better) with the Gloop and then tying them off. You need four hands for this so find a helper. Have the helper put 2 fingers of each hand into the opening of a balloon to stretch it WIDE while you add the Gloop. Try to get all the air out before you tie it.

3. Record your observations and questions in drawings and in words. Make a list of physical properties that Gloop has. *Physical properties* are traits of appearance and behavior including color, texture, strength, stretchiness, density, bounciness, flowability, and so on.

4. When you are ready to put the Gloop away, place it in a zip top bag and store it in the refrigerator. It will keep a week or more and is good to use until it starts to grow mold.

Vocabulary and concepts appear on page 153.

Observations, Ideas, Sketches, Questions

THINGS I TRIED	OBSERVATIONS

Physical Properties of Gloop:

25. T-shirt Designs

Use your Radiant Color skills (see page 52) to produce awesome T-shirts for wearing or gift giving.

WARNING: Evaporated rubbing alcohol can cause headaches. Work in an area with good air flow and avoid breathing the vapor.

> If you have made mistakes . . . there is always another chance for you . . . . for this thing we call "failure" is not the falling down, but the staying down.
> —Mary Pickford

Materials

Old rag T-shirts, for practicing patterns
Plain, white or pastel, prewashed 100%
   cotton T-shirt or boxer shorts
Permanent markers, several colors
Rubbing alcohol

Eye dropper
1 large coffee can, food storage container,
   or cup
1 large rubber band
An iron

I. Create Your Shirt

1. If you haven't done "Radiant Color," go back and do that activity first.
2. Plan the shirt's design and color scheme. Your design can be composed of disks of color, tiny to large, but doesn't have to be. You can make a continuous border at the collar and/or sleeves. Even letters can be spread with careful placement of the alcohol drips.
3. Practice your plan on a rag to make sure it works well. This is a very helpful step!
4. Place the area of the shirt to be worked on (single thickness) over the container and secure with a rubber band so the fabric lies flat.
5. Apply marker colors as planned for that area.
6. Slowly drip alcohol from the dropper onto the shirt to spread the design as desired. Use gravity to help you spread the color more in one direction, when needed, by turning the can on its side. Allow the area to dry.
7. Move a new area of the shirt to the container opening and repeat the process until you have completed your plan.
8. After the shirt is all dry, bond the color to the cotton by pressing your design with an iron. Use the "Cotton" setting.
9. Repeated washings, hot water, and strong detergents will cause marker colors to fade. Wash in cold water and gentle detergent for best results.

Vocabulary and concepts appear on page 155.

Observations, Ideas, Sketches, Questions

Designs Before Alcohol:

Did you hear about the man who fell into an upholstery machine? He's fully recovered.

Designs After Alcohol:

VOCABULARY AND CONCEPTS

1. It's a Gas

Vocabulary

Hydrogen peroxide: H_2O_2; an acid: a water solution of it is used to kill germs on cuts

Oxygen: O_2; produced by plants as they build food molecules during photosynthesis; used by plants and animal cells to release energy from foods

Carbon dioxide: CO_2; produced in plant and animal cells when energy is released from foods; also a product of most burning reactions

Chemical reaction: the production of a new substance or substances

Decompose: to break down chemically into simpler substances

Enzyme: a group of substances found in cells that speed up certain chemical reactions

Chemical equation: the symbolic way to write what occurs in a chemical reaction

Reactants: the substances that take part in a chemical reaction

Products: the substances that result from a chemical reaction

What's Going On?

You are a chemist! You have just carried out several chemical reactions that produced substances that were not there when you started. Congratulations!

You may have used hydrogen peroxide before to kill germs on cuts. Hydrogen peroxide is chemically fragile. Quite a few substances, including enzymes in your cut flesh, can make it fall apart or decompose into water and oxygen gas. In Part I, the hydrogen peroxide decomposes with the help of an enzyme in the yeast.

The bubbles that form are made of oxygen gas. The following equation is a quick way of writing out what happens.

hydrogen peroxide $\rightarrow$ water + **oxygen gas**

$$2\ H_2O_2 \quad \rightarrow \quad 2\ H_2O \quad + \quad O_2$$

Oxygen gas, as you know, is needed for life. Your cells use it in the chemical reaction that releases energy from food. Oxygen is also needed for fire. Normal air is only about 20% oxygen. When you place your match near the decomposing hydrogen peroxide, the flame gets extra oxygen and burns brighter. The extra oxygen also causes glowing wood to ignite into flame. An unknown gas with the same results would surely be oxygen.

In Part II, carbon dioxide is made in the chemical reaction between vinegar and baking soda. The following equation represents what happens.

		baking soda	$\rightarrow$	water	+	sodium acetate	+	carbon dioxide gas
vinegar	+	$NaHCO_3$	$\rightarrow$	H_2O	+	$NaC_2H_3O_2$	+	CO_2
$HC_2H_3O_2$								

A flame goes out immediately in the carbon dioxide since no oxygen is present to allow burning. A glowing splint darkens for the same reason. An unknown gas that has the same flame and splint results *might* be carbon dioxide. Some other gases will have similar results.

Air and Other Gases / Explosion!

The Mystery Gases?

The mystery gases are, in fact, both carbon dioxide. In both cases, the flame goes out immediately and the glowing splint dims.

Are you surprised that yeast can produce oxygen in one case and carbon dioxide in another? In sugar water, the yeast cells break down the sugar to get energy for growth. Carbon dioxide is a waste product of the process. This process takes longer than the reaction between yeast and hydrogen peroxide because the sugar is only used gradually by the cells as they grow and divide. The yeast cells continue to grow and to produce carbon dioxide as long as the sugar supply holds out. The card or plate helps keep the room air from mixing with the carbon dioxide. Even though carbon dioxide is denser than air and therefore tends to sink, different gases mix quickly with one another when amounts are small.

2. Explosion!

Vocabulary

Explosion: bursting outward suddenly

Chemical reaction: recombining substances so that one or more new substances are formed

Product: a new substance formed by a chemical reaction

Pressure: a push distributed over a certain area

Carbon dioxide: the gas you produce as a waste product of "burning" foods; released through the lungs. Carbon dioxide is a product of most instances of burning. Plants use this gas with water to build food molecules. It has the formula

CO_2, which tells you that each particle is made of one atom of carbon attached to two atoms of oxygen.

Friction: resistance to motion when surfaces touch

What's Going On?

The dry ingredients in the Alka Seltzer tablet react chemically with one another once they are placed in water. Chemical reactions produce new substances and one of the new substances formed in this case is carbon dioxide gas. The particles that make up a gas are fast moving compared to the particles in a solid or a liquid, so the pressure inside the film can builds. When the pressure inside the can gets high enough, it suddenly overcomes the friction holding the cap in place, and the cap shoots off. The Fuji brand caps fit very tightly, so the pressure gets quite high before the cap moves. This high pressure provides enough force for the cap to have an impressive flight.

Whether you were casually exploring or actually experimenting, you may have found

some of the following relationships. Adding weight to the cap results in shorter "flights." The more weight an object has, the less it accelerates from a given force. Neither the amount of water nor the amount of Alka Seltzer affect cap flights since the cap pops off at a certain pressure. However, more water or more Alka Seltzer can shorten the *time* it takes for the explosion to occur since reaction time depends on the amount of the surface contact between the substances reacting. Hotter water also speeds up the reaction, whereas colder water slows it down. Since the caps and can sizes vary slightly, some caps will fit more tightly than others and will therefore allow a higher build-up of pressure before they pop.

3. Implosion!

Vocabulary

Implosion: a sudden inward bursting
States of matter: gas, liquid, and solid
Boiling: changing from a liquid to a gas caused by heating
Condensing: changing from a gas to a liquid caused by cooling
Fluid pressure: the push per unit area of a gas or a liquid. Fluid pressure is exerted in all directions.
Air pressure: the fluid pressure of the air due to the weight of the air above. Air pressure decreases as altitude increases.
Kinetic energy: the energy objects have when they are moving. Energy is the ability to do work.

What's Going On?

Boiling the water in the can produces steam, which is water in the gas state. The steam pushes the air out of the can and extra steam escapes the can as well. All matter is made of tiny, tiny particles. The particles of steam that now fill the can, being so hot, are very fast moving. They have lots of kinetic energy. Although they are farther apart from one another than the cooler air particles outside the can, they move faster, so the steam particles collide against the can's walls with about the same pressure as the air on the outside.

When the can is put into the cold water, the steam cools. Cooling is a loss of energy. Once cooled, the steam particles are no longer so fast moving. In fact, they condense back into the liquid state where they are quite close together. Particles in the liquid state are many, many times closer together than particles in the gas state.

A can full of steam produces only a drop of liquid water. This small amount of water cannot exert much pressure on the inside walls of the can. With hardly anything pushing out from the inside, the can is crushed by the air pressure outside pushing in.

Water from the bowl moves into the opening in the can while this is going on, but before much water has moved in, the can is already crushed by the air pressure. The sudden collapsing of an object toward its center is called an *implosion*. Air pressure is powerful!

Note that suction is an idea that leads to misunderstanding. Suction implies a pull, but neither gases nor liquids can pull. (The term is as sensible as saying to your sister when she punches you, "My face sure sucked in your fist!") What we call suction is really a situation in which there are two different pressures. The so-called "sucking" action of drinking straws, eye droppers, suction cups, and hurricanes occurs because a nearby fluid at higher pressure is moving naturally to an area of lower pressure. Matter is made of particles and all that particles can do is bounce around and *push* the objects they hit. They can push with more force or less force, but they cannot pull.

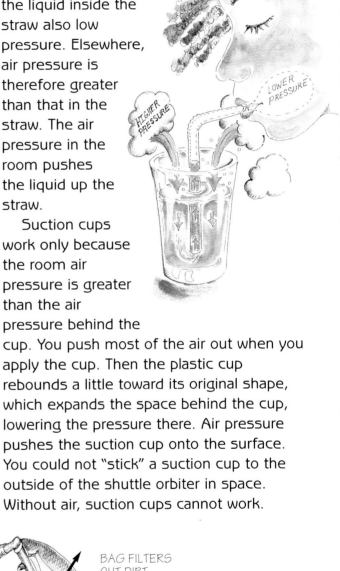

A drinking straw works by exactly the same principle. You shape your mouth to create a low pressure zone above the straw. The air in the straw moves to the low pressure area, which makes the area above the liquid inside the straw also low pressure. Elsewhere, air pressure is therefore greater than that in the straw. The air pressure in the room pushes the liquid up the straw.

Suction cups work only because the room air pressure is greater than the air pressure behind the cup. You push most of the air out when you apply the cup. Then the plastic cup rebounds a little toward its original shape, which expands the space behind the cup, lowering the pressure there. Air pressure pushes the suction cup onto the surface. You could not "stick" a suction cup to the outside of the shuttle orbiter in space. Without air, suction cups cannot work.

Where Else Do You See Air Pressure in Action?

Can you list some everyday objects that require air pressure changes to function? A vacuum cleaner uses a fan to create a low pressure area inside the machine. Room air is at higher pressure so it rushes toward the low pressure area through the hose. Dirt and dust get swept along in the wind caused by the moving air and are caught in a filter.

4. Instant Meringue

Vocabulary

Citric acid: A common food ingredient. Like other acids, it tastes sour.

Polymer: a large molecule made of a long chain of smaller units

Protein: one category of polymers found in living things. Hair, nails, and muscle are high in protein. Egg whites are about 10% protein.

Denatured protein: a protein molecule that has had a change in its three-dimensional shape

What's Going On?

Egg white is about 90% water and 10% protein. The protein molecules, though very large as molecules go, start out as compact blobs that are small enough to dissolve in the water. When the baking soda and citric acid come in contact with one another, they react chemically to produce carbon dioxide gas. (This reaction is very similar to the one between baking soda and vinegar.) The tiny gas bubbles that form are trapped by the egg white and, along with the acid, they transform the structure of the protein molecules into a new three-dimensional shape that is looser and larger. Now the protein will not dissolve in the water. Instead, it forms a semi-solid net that gives the meringue shape and holds the well-dispersed water and gas bubbles in place. The change in the structure of the protein molecules is called *denaturing*.

Doubling the amount of egg white results in a denser foam that may have a smaller volume than otherwise. Adding sugar has no noticeable effect on the foam. Substituting flour for baking soda, however, makes a big difference. With flour, no chemical reaction occurs and no foam is produced at all.

5. Your Dear Friend, Egbert

Vocabulary

Volume: space occupied

Density: the mass or weight of an object compared to its volume; how compact a substance or object is

Buoyancy: the upward force on an object in a fluid

Water displacement: when water is moved out of the way by an object

Force: a push or a pull

Archimedes' Principle: the buoyant force on an object is equal to the weight of the fluid displaced

Solution: a mixture of at least one substance dissolved in another

What's Going On?

Fresh water, salt water, and Egbert differ from one another in a property called *density*. Density is how compact matter is, or, in other words, how much weight there is in a certain amount of space. For example, marshmallows have a low density whereas lead has a high density. Density determines what will float and what will sink. More dense substances sink in less dense liquids. A fresh egg is a little more dense than plain water so it sinks. When salt is added to water, particles of salt move in between water particles, making the salt water more dense.

The salt water is a little more dense than the egg, so in salt water, the egg floats. When fresh water is carefully dribbled on top of salt water, there is little mixing of the two types of water. The result is layers of water with the fresh water floating on top of the salt water. Since Egbert floats on the salt water but sinks in the fresh water, he rides right in the middle of the two liquid layers.

The previous explanation may not be good enough for you. If you are wondering why density differences determine what floats and what sinks, you might want to learn about the buoyant force. Read on.

Buoyancy

A force is a push or a pull. Water (and every fluid) will exert an upward force on objects that are put into it because water pressure increases with depth. The strength of this buoyant force is equal to the weight of the water that was moved out of the way by the

— Fresh water is less dense.

— Egbert's density is in the middle.

— Salt water is more dense.

object. (That's Archimedes' Principle.) An object that weighs less than an equal volume of water will be pushed up until it floats. An amount of water equal in size to the part of the floating object that is under water weighs the same as the entire object. If a floating object just barely rises above the water's surface, its density is very close to that of water. If it floats high in the water, its density is a lot less than the water. Any object that weighs more than an equal volume of water will sink.

If a liquid such as salt water is more dense than water, then its buoyant force is greater and more dense objects can be supported by it.

fresh water

salt water

slightly less dense

much less dense

more dense

Where Else Do You See Buoyancy in Action?

Lifting things that are in water is easier than lifting them in air. Did you ever bring up a boat's anchor? While the anchor is in the water, the water's buoyant force helps you lift it out, so it feels light. Once the anchor is out of the water, all of its weight is supported by you, so it feels heavy.

Boats are shaped to displace a lot of water in order to have enough buoyant force exerted on them by the water to float. Have you ever wondered how a cruise ship, carrying many people, stays afloat? That's a lot of buoyancy!

Did you know that you float higher in ocean water than in fresh water?

Barges and freighters ride high in the water when empty and low in the water when full.

6. Rainbow in a Drinking Straw

Vocabulary

Density: mass per unit volume; how compact matter is

Solution: a mixture of at least one substance dissolved in another

Concentration: a comparison of the amount of substance dissolved in a solution to the amount of liquid doing the dissolving. In the case of salt water, it is the weight of salt compared to the weight of water in the solution. If there is more salt, the solution is more concentrated.

Miscible: combines; water and alcohol are miscible

Immiscible: stays separate; water and oil are immiscible

Viscosity: resistance to flow; the more viscous a fluid, the slower it flows

What's Going On?

In each of the three stacking activities, only one sequence will stack. The stacking sequence is determined by density. If a more dense solution is added on top of a less dense one, the more dense one sinks through the other, mixing the two together as it goes. However, if the second solution is less dense, it floats on top and blending occurs only slightly where they meet. Gentle technique and the small contact area in the straw help keep the mixing to a minimum.

Solution Stacking: From most dense to least dense, bottom to top, the sequence is shampoo (blue), salt water (red), fresh water (yellow), alcohol (green).

Concentration Stacking: Most dense is the solution d, with the most salt. The sequence bottom to top is d, c, b, a. Use the secret record to compare your color results.

Temperature Stacking: Most dense is the cold water. Bottom to top the sequence is cold (blue), room temperature (green), warm (yellow), hot (red). The temperatures start to equalize right away so some mixing occurs at the boundaries and they are not very distinct.

If the above results differ from your own, likely sources of error are contamination from mixing up the eye droppers, not shaking/drying out the straw well between tries, and, in the case of temperature stacking, waiting too long.

If undisturbed, the solution stack will take over a week to completely blend. The concentration and temperature stacks blend within a few days.

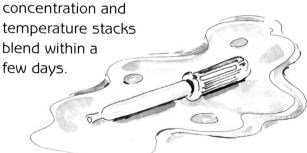

If you try these activities in something wider than a straw, such as a drinking glass, it is difficult, if not impossible, for stacking to occur. The area of contact between substances is too great and mixing dominates over the density difference. Of all the substances used, shampoo is the only one that will stay separate for a while this way.

The density column described in #3 of "Exploration Ideas" works so well because the oil is not miscible with either water or alcohol. The syrup will mix with water if stirred well, but it has *both* viscosity and density working to keep it separate. As the days and weeks go by, you will see the syrup/water boundary blur while the boundaries on either side of the oil stay totally distinct.

7. Ice and Oil:

Would Icebergs Have Been a Problem If the *Titanic* Had Sailed on Oil?

Vocabulary

Surface area: total area of the exposed surfaces of an object
Density: mass per unit volume; how compact an object or substance is
Repel: push away

What's Going On?

Icebergs would *still* have been a problem if the *Titanic* had sailed on oil. In fact, because even more of the ice would have been below the surface of the water, icebergs would have been even harder to see and avoid.

What you've been watching is a density change happening right in front of your eyes! The melting ice becomes more dense when it turns into liquid. Density is how compact a substance is. The molecules of water in the liquid state are more closely packed than the molecules of water in the solid state (ice). Substances that are more dense sink in substances that are less dense.

The ice cube is just a little *less* dense than the oil and so it floats. As the ice warms, however, it melts, and melted ice, water, is *more* dense than oil. It collects at the bottom of the ice cube until a drop separates from the ice and slowly falls to the bottom of the glass. The nature of oil molecules and water molecules cause them to repel one another and this leads to the spherical shape the water takes. A sphere has the smallest surface area for its volume of all shapes. When the water is in a ball, the least possible contact occurs between the water and the oil.

Something curious happens when the ice cube gets quite small. Before it is entirely melted it, too, will sink. The reason why has to do with another aspect of surface area. Small bits of matter have more surface area compared to their volume than larger pieces. The surface of the ice is in the liquid state and when the piece of the ice is very small, the greater density of this liquid makes the average density of ice-plus-water high enough to exceed the density of the oil. In other words, for its size, a little piece of ice carries a lot of dense liquid water on its back and this makes it sink.

It is interesting to note that water is an oddity. Other substances (with the exception of bismuth) get less dense when they melt so the solid state sinks in its liquid. A gold ring will sink in a pot of melted gold (until it melts). Water is just the opposite and it's lucky for us that it is. If water were like other substances and ice sank, lakes in the north would freeze solid in the winter. Ice would form on the surface of the water, then sink. More ice would form, which would sink, and no ice layer would ever insulate the rest of the water from the cold air. As it is, in areas where lakes do freeze, the layer of ice on the surface insulates the water underneath from further freezing and in the spring, higher temperatures at the surface melt the ice away. Fish and other aquatic life thus survive year round. Being an oddity can be a good thing!

Where Else Do You See Density in Action?

Hot air balloons go up and down
Ships float and sink
Salad dressing forms layers in the bottle
Submarines submerge and surface
Earth's crustal plates move as the fluid mantle below rises and sinks

Oil is less dense than vinegar so it floats.

Vinegar is more dense than oil so it sinks.

8. Pop Bottle Magic

Vocabulary

Volume: an amount of space occupied
Mass: the amount of matter in an object
Density: the mass of an object compared to its volume; how compact a substance or object is
Compressibility: the ability to shrink when under pressure
Ballast tanks: containers of water on a submarine that can be filled or emptied to control surfacing and submerging

What's Going On?

Solids, liquids, and gases differ from one another in how compressible they are. When liquids or solids are squeezed, they will shrink in size, but only a very small amount. Gases, on the other hand, are *very* compressible. In fact, if you double the pressure on a gas, its volume will drop to one half of what it was. Squeezing the bottle in this activity puts pressure on everything inside the bottle; the water, the air, and the glass and rubber of the droppers. Of these items, only the air is noticeably compressed. As the air inside a dropper shrinks in size, water moves into its place. You can see the water move up into the dropper when you squeeze the bottle.

The extra water increases the mass of the dropper without changing its volume. More mass in the same space means the dropper has become more dense. If it becomes more dense than the surrounding water, it sinks. Since you had set up the droppers to be just slightly less dense than the water in the first place, a little squeeze increases their densities enough for them to sink.

The sequence of colors in Part II is very reliable because each colored dropper started out at a different density. The fullest, most dense dropper sinks first. The other droppers, in turn, each need a slightly harder squeeze to sink.

A submarine operates in a very similar way. Sea water is pumped into or out of containers called ballast tanks to adjust the average density of the sub. The submarine sinks or floats according to the amount of water in the tanks.

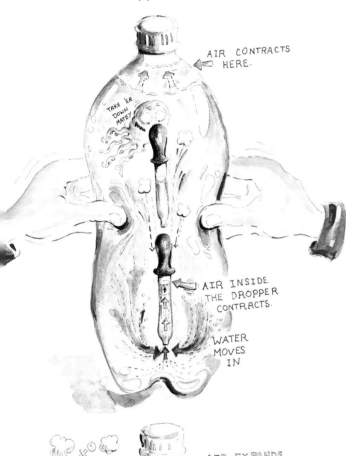

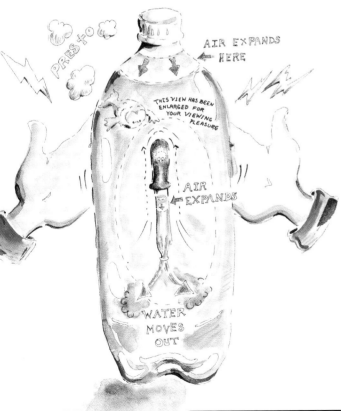

9. Bernoulli's Blast I:
Give Me a Lift

Vocabulary

Force: a push or pull

Air pressure: the force of air on a certain area

Lift: the upward force on an airplane wing or other object due to a difference in air pressure below and above

Bernoulli's Principle: still air (or other fluid) exerts more pressure around it than that around a stream of moving air

Fluid: a liquid or a gas

Balanced forces: when opposing forces on an object are equal in size; the result is no change in the motion of the object

Unbalanced forces: when opposing forces on an object are unequal; the result is a change in motion

What's Going On?

Air exerts pressure in every direction all the time. Bernoulli figured out that *moving* air (or other fluid) pushes less at right angles to the direction of its flow than still or more slowly moving air. This idea, called Bernoulli's Principle, explains why the water rose up in the straw. The faster the blast of moving air from your mouth, the lower the pressure exerted *around* the blast (even though it puts lots of pressure on objects in its path). Since the blast flows across the top of the lower straw, the pressure on the liquid in that straw is reduced. Elsewhere on the water's surface the air pressure is normal (higher in comparison), so the water is pushed upward through the upright straw toward the low pressure area. This unbalanced upward force is called *lift*. When the water gets up *into* the air stream, it is then pushed and scattered by the quickly moving air.

Applying the same idea to the ball in the cup, blowing across the top of the cup will produce lift on the ball and the ball will pop up out of the cup when the air speed is high enough. The rule given was you "may not touch the ball with any solid or liquid object." Air is a gas so it is allowed! Controlling the ball's motion to get it to land in the second cup is not easy! Succeeding twice in ten tries is good and four in ten tries probably qualifies you for national distinction.

Airplane wings make flight possible due to the same principle. Each airplane wing moving through the air splits the air stream and forces the air above the wing to travel over a curved surface while the air below follows a straight and therefore shorter path. The air above the wing covers its longer path in the same time as the air below and so must travel faster. The more quickly moving air above the wing exerts less pressure than the slower-moving air below, resulting in an upward force. When speeds are great enough, the upward force on the wing is larger than the downward force of gravity and the airplane climbs.

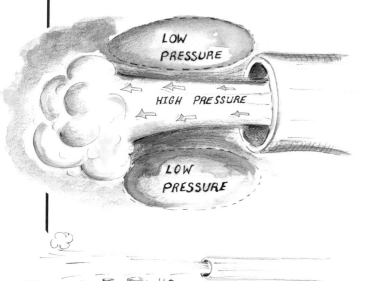

While the plane is cruising, the forces of lift and gravity are balanced and the plane stays at the same altitude. To increase or decrease lift, the pilot can adjust either the speed of the plane or the position of its wing flaps.

One last point about Bernoulli's Principle is that it doesn't matter at all whether it is the air or the wing that is moving. Imagine a toy airplane on a string. Whether a child runs with it or stands still holding it in a breeze, the movement of air across the wings gives it lift.

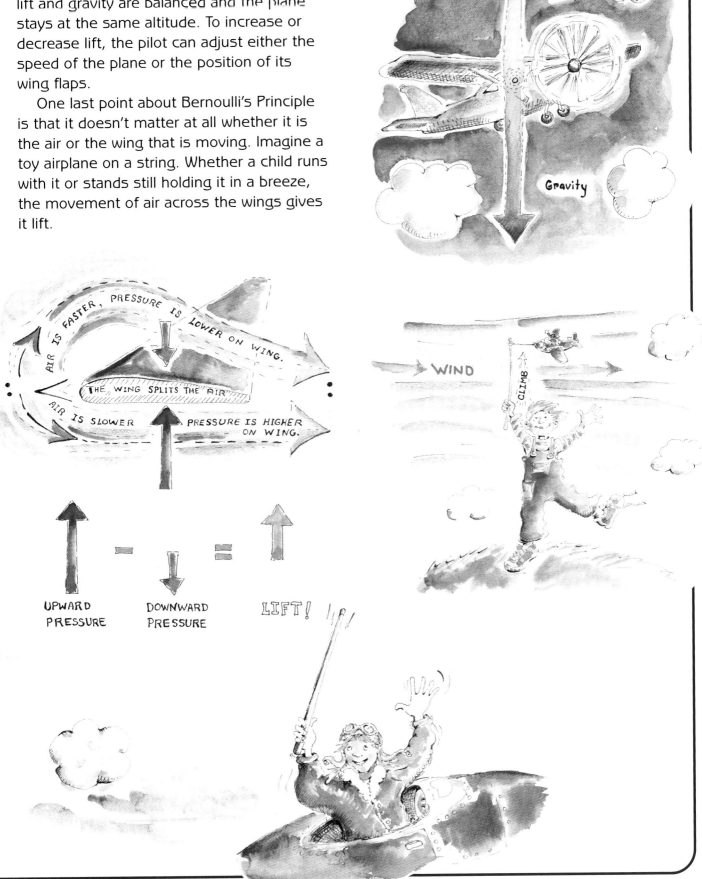

Lift

Gravity

AIR IS FASTER, PRESSURE IS LOWER ON WING.

THE WING SPLITS THE AIR

AIR IS SLOWER　　PRESSURE IS HIGHER ON WING.

UPWARD PRESSURE　−　DOWNWARD PRESSURE　=　LIFT!

WIND

CLIMB

10. Bernoulli's Blast II:

No Visible Means of Support

Vocabulary

Force: a push or pull

Air pressure: the force of air on a certain area

Balanced forces: when opposing forces on an object are equal in size; results in no change in the motion of the object

Unbalanced forces: when opposing forces on an object are unequal; results in a change in motion

Bernoulli's Principle: still air (or other fluid) exerts more pressure around it than that around a stream of moving air

Fluid: a liquid or a gas

Lift: the upward force on an airplane wing or other object due to a difference in air pressure above and below

What's Going On?

With the cereal and the Ping-Pong ball, it's not so surprising that they are held up by the air stream. The balls stay roughly at the same height because forces upward and downward on the ball are balanced. When a ball is hovering, the downward force of gravity balances the upward force of the air from the dryer. With these balanced forces acting on the ball, the ball moves neither up nor down.

The wobbling of the ball is due to turbulence and inconsistencies of the air stream. This is where the situation gets interesting. Notice that the ball often moves to one side out of the center of the air stream. Just when it looks as though the ball should fall out of the stream, something

seems to push it back to center. Watch this happen.

Why isn't the ball pushed totally out of the air stream? Good question! That's where Bernoulli's Principle comes in. This principle, for most people, is what you might call a "counter-intuitive" phenomenon. In other words, it seems to go against logic. Here's how it works . . .

Air exerts pressure in every direction all the time. Bernoulli figured out that *moving* air (or other fluid) pushes less at right angles to the direction of its flow than still or more slowly moving air. To apply this to the hovering balls: when the ball moves to the edge of the air stream, the faster moving air in the stream pushes outward on the ball less than the air in the room pushes it inward. As a result of these unbalanced forces, the ball is pushed back into the air stream.

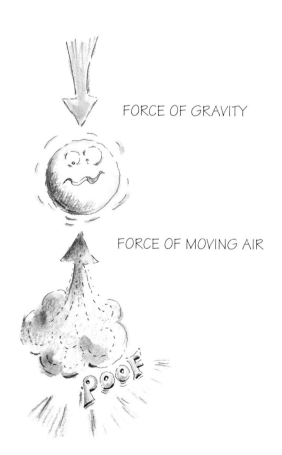

FORCE OF GRAVITY

FORCE OF MOVING AIR

POOF

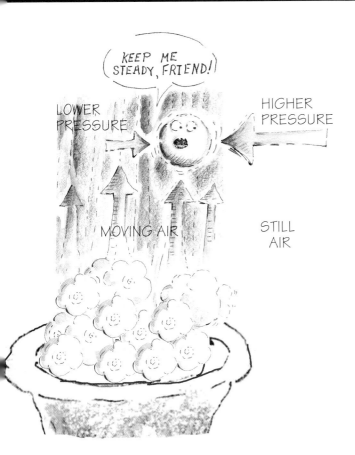

KEEP ME
STEADY, FRIEND!

LOWER
PRESSURE

HIGHER
PRESSURE

MOVING AIR

STILL
AIR

With the funnel and ball, the situation is slightly more complicated and even more surprising. In this case *two* forces act on the ball in the downward direction: gravity and the direct force of the blowing air. Yet, if you blow hard enough, the moving air over the top side of the ball results in such low air pressure that normal air pressure below the ball is a stronger force than both of the downward forces put together. The result is a net force in the upward direction and the ball stays in the funnel.

Where Else Do You See Bernoulli's Principle in Action?

Shower curtains blow in toward you during your shower.

Things in your car blow out the window when the car is going fast.

Fireplace chimneys draw better when the wind is blowing.

11. Radiant Color

Vocabulary

Solubility: ability to dissolve

Cohesion: attraction to self

Adhesion: attraction to another substance

Capillary action: the movement of a liquid through tiny openings in a solid

Chromatography: a method of separating substances in a mixture

Solvent: a substance that dissolves other substances

Qualitative: relates to information described in words. Example: "large" is a qualitative observation.

Quantitative: relates to information in the form of numbers from measurements. Example: "798 pounds" is a quantitative observation.

What's Going On?

With most pens, the filter paper ends up with bands of different colors from the original ink color. Most inks are not just one color but are mixtures of several colored substances combined. Since the colors are different substances, they each have their own characteristics, and you have taken advantage of this to pull them apart. Black is usually the most complex color mixture and so is an especially good color ink to use.

The process starts with the water moving up the paper wick and along the paper disk due to something called *capillary action.*

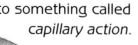

The adhesion of the water to the paper moves the water along the paper a tiny distance. The strong cohesion of the water pulls trailing water along the same distance and the process continues. As the water moves this way across the paper disk, water-soluble (dissolvable) parts of the ink mixture move along with it. The water and the paper tug on each colored substance with varying strengths. Accordingly, each colored substance moves at its own rate. One color may move along almost as fast as the water, other colors lag behind the first, and others may only move slightly. The flow of each color compared to the flow of the water is a signature of that substance. And the combination of color bands that appear is a signature of a certain ink recipe.

This method of separating substances from a mixture is called chromatography. It is used in laboratories that analyze samples of mixtures. Food chemists, medical researchers, plant scientists, crime scientists, and others often need to figure out the contents of samples they collect. The first step to identifying unknown substances is to separate them. Sometimes water is used as the solvent, but often a different liquid is used. Usually something other than paper is used to do the absorbing. When the mixed substances do not differ in color, the chromatogram may be treated with chemicals to bring out colors.

Your investigation results depend on the ink that you used. There are about as many recipes for a color of ink as there are brands so that, for the most part, each pen produces a unique chromatogram. If you had an unlabeled ink sample, you could identify it by making a chromatogram from it, then comparing it to chromatograms made from many brands of that color. For any ink recipe, the pigments that move at all will bunch up together when they reach the rim of the paper. The water evaporates but the pigments stay on the paper. The shape of the paper makes no difference in the appearance of the chromatogram until the pigments reach the rim. Food colors separate like the pen colors do whether they are first mixed together or not. Hot water travels along the paper faster than cold water.

12. Whack It!

Vocabulary

Mass: the amount of matter in an object; related to but not the same as weight

Inertia: resistance to a change in motion; inertia varies with mass; the more mass an object has, the more force it takes to change the object's motion

Force: a push or a pull

Acceleration: while commonly used to mean speeding up, in physics it means *any* change in motion; speeding up, slowing down, or turning

Newton's Second Law of Motion: the acceleration of an object depends on the force put on the object and on the mass of the object; acceleration = force/mass

What's Going On?

When the ruler whacks the card, the card shoots out away from the ruler. The tube, which was resting on the card, moves away as well. The golf ball, however, always lands in the cup, directly below where it started. When a foam or Ping-Pong ball is used instead of a golf ball, it *rarely* lands in the cup. The difference in the two cases is the masses of the balls. The golf ball has much more mass than the Ping-Pong ball. With more mass, the golf ball has more inertia, so it resists a change in motion more. It takes more force to move the golf ball than to move the Ping-Pong ball the same amount. The little force exerted by the tilting tube moves the Ping-Pong ball toward you as it falls, enough that it misses the cup. The golf ball, however, moves toward you very little in the time it takes to fall, and so lands in the cup. This demonstration reflects Isaac Newton's Second Law of Motion, acceleration = force/mass. Realize that in a fraction, the *smaller* the value of the denominator, (the bottom), the *bigger* the value of the fraction. Therefore, a small mass accelerates more from a given force than a large mass.

The water in the cup cushions, or softens, the landing of the ball and egg. This prevents the ball from bouncing out and prevents the egg from cracking.

MASS OF GOLF BALL RESISTS THE SMALL PUSH OF THE TUBE

SMALLER MASS OF THE PING-PONG BALL CANNOT RESIST SIDEWAYS PUSH OF TUBE

WATCH THE OVER-FLOW

SMALL FORCE SMALL MASS... I CAN RELATE!

You should be able to do several cup/tube/golf balls at a time. The taller the tube used, and the narrower the cup, the more perfect the alignment needs to be for success.

13. Be a Swinger!

Vocabulary

Inertia: resistance to a change in motion. Objects at rest tend to stay at rest and objects in motion tend to continue at a constant speed in a straight line (Sir Isaac Newton's First Law of Motion).

Force: a push or a pull

Friction: a force opposing motion when objects touch

What's Going On?

Why don't the cup and water fall when the tray is upside down?

The tray, the cup, and the water, like all objects, have inertia. An object that is moving *keeps moving*. And it keeps moving at a steady speed in a straight line until a force speeds it up, slows it down, or turns it. The pull of the cord provides a force that keeps the tray and its contents moving in a circle rather than a straight line.

Why doesn't the cup slide on the tray?

The motion of the cup away from you and the force of you pulling back on the tray cause the tray and the cup to *push on each other*. These forces increase the friction between them that keeps the cup from sliding. If the tray is not moving quickly enough, the cup, the water, and the tray will fall. The faster you swing them, the heavier

they feel and the greater the friction keeping the cup from sliding.

If you investigated smaller sizes of swingers, you probably found that while they work pretty much the same, you can rotate the swinger from your wrist or fingertips instead of from your shoulder. The shorter the distance from the center of rotation to the tray, the higher the needed rate of rotation. It's easier to swing short and light swingers faster. A tiny swinger made from a film canister top and thread can be swung faster than you can count.

Where Else Do You See These Principles in Action?

In the washing machine, your socks are flung to the walls of the washer during the spin cycle.

A type of amusement park ride swings people around in a circle such that when the floor drops down below their feet, they stay in place on the wall.

The moon and other satellites orbit Earth and Earth orbits the sun. Instead of a cord, the connecting force is gravity. Inertia explains why the moon and Earth keep going; it's natural! The force of gravity curves the otherwise straight path. If an orbiting body like the moon were to slow down significantly, it would eventually crash into Earth.

Space station designers have considered using rotation to simulate gravity. The station itself would rotate and the astronauts would be like the cup on your tray. Instead of floating around with no up or down, "up" would be toward the center of rotation and "down" would be toward the outside. Such a design would have benefits for astronauts but has not been practical to build.

Riding in a car without a seat belt is dangerous because of your own inertia. If the driver slams on the brakes, you continue moving in a straight line until something such as the windshield changes your motion (and remodels your face!).

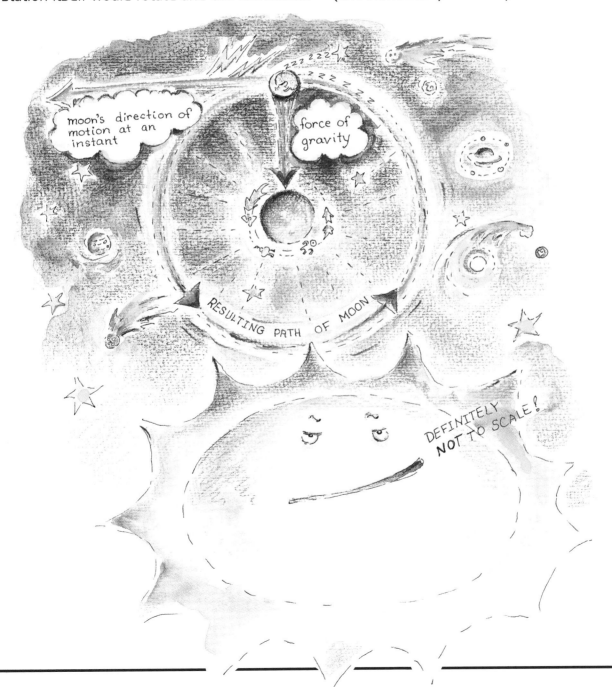

14. What If Gravity Disappeared?

A Workout for Your Brain

Vocabulary

Mass: amount of matter. *Mass* and *weight* are often used interchangeably but that is not quite right. Weight is a force and depends on gravity. Mass just depends on how much matter there is, how many atoms are present. You weigh less on the moon, but your mass stays the same.

Gravity: an attraction between any two objects caused by their masses. It is only noticeable when at least one of the objects is huge, such as a planet, a moon, or a star. The bigger the masses of the objects, the greater the attraction. The greater the distances between the centers of the objects, the smaller the attraction.

Zero gravity: a misleading term that is used to describe the conditions astronauts experience when they are in orbit.

Objects don't fall to the floor of the cabin and objects put on a scale show no weight. These conditions occur because the space craft and all its belongings are in continuous free fall. Gravity does pull the space craft toward Earth, but because of its speed and distance from the ground, its curving fall runs parallel to the surface of Earth and the ship gets no closer to the ground. You experience an instant of the free fall feeling on certain amusement park rides and when an elevator starts down quickly. The term *zero gravity* also can be used to describe the *almost* nonexistent force of gravity in deep space, great distances from any planet or star.

Convection: the natural movement of a heated gas or liquid; warmed sections become less dense and rise, while cooler sections are more dense and sink; only occurs in gravity

Diffusion: the drifting of one gas or liquid through another as the natural bouncing of the particles mixes them; occurs with or without gravity

What's Going On?

ACTION	HOW CHANGED IF GRAVITY DISAPPEARED
Walking	Very different! You have no weight without gravity. If you push off normally with one foot you are likely to push yourself away from the ground. Nothing will pull you back so, for your next step, you'll have nothing from which to push off. You could use your hands to pull your weightless self from place to place. Indoors, you could easily push off the floor to any part of the room. Zigzag from wall to wall to ceiling. Please clean the cobwebs at the ceiling while you are there! Outdoors, there would be great danger of pushing away from the ground and drifting off forever.
Taking a bath	City water systems work by using gravity to deliver water from a water tower to peoples' homes. The water gets its pressure from starting up high. Without gravity, water would not come out of the faucet. If you had a pump to push it out, you could get water, but it would be impossible to keep it in the tub. As the water hit the tub, it would splash back up and keep on going until it hit the walls where some would stick and some would continue bouncing around the room. Messy!
Writing a letter	Pencil and paper would work fine. Some pens would quit delivering ink, though, without gravity to pull the ink downward in a continuous flow.
Riding a bicycle	Impossible. You'd need help to get on the bike in a "normal" position. Once on, you could ride all you wanted but you'd have a tough time going anywhere. You would have no traction at all. The first little bump would push you and the bike off the ground. Without the tires pushing back on the ground, the bike cannot go forward. On the other hand, it sure would be easy to pedal and you could do awesome stunts!
Tossing a tennis ball	You can toss the ball just fine. If you want a friend to catch it, however, your "normal" aim will make the ball go too high. If your friend misses it and you are outside, you may never see the ball again. Instead of hitting the ground and quickly coming to a stop, it will continue moving on a straight path. If you miss a catch indoors, the ball will bounce back and forth off the ceiling, walls, and floor, slowing down only slightly as it goes because of air resistance.

(continued on following page)

(continued from preceding page)

ACTION	HOW CHANGED IF GRAVITY DISAPPEARED
Mixing cookie dough	An electric mixer will work normally, but you will be challenged to keep track of the food. Some of the ingredients will stick to others and the bowl, but some bits will swirl up and out. You will get a spreading white cloud when you add dry flour to the dough.
Using a thermometer	The thermometer will work normally. It works due to expansion and contraction of the fluid inside and does not depend on gravity.
Shooting a squirt gun	When filled with water, the gun will work normally. It has a little pump inside that pushes the water out. Once out, the water will travel in straight lines similar to the tennis ball. Some water may stick to a target and some will bounce off. As the water supply inside decreases, a mixture of water and air will squirt out instead of just water as there is nothing to keep the water at the bottom by the squirt tube.
Drinking orange juice	You had better use a juice box and straw to keep the juice contained but once you swallow, the juice will go to your stomach just fine. Muscles in the wall of your esophagus (throat) squeeze food and drink along in the right direction with or without gravity's help.
Doing sit-ups	Doing these works fine, but since you have no weight, it's awfully easy. You'll get bored before you get tired and it will not be easy to build strength.
Using the toilet	Remember the mess made by taking a bath? Using the toilet will require special measures! On the space shuttle, astronauts use a specially designed toilet with a vacuum system. All wastes are suctioned into the toilet so they don't bounce around the room. Good idea, eh?
Sleeping	You won't stay on a bed so a mattress has no use. You had better hook up somewhere, though, so you don't bump into something or "sleep-float" right off the planet. While you sleep, your arms naturally extend out in front of you, relaxed at the wrists and elbows.

(continued on facing page)

ACTION	HOW CHANGED IF GRAVITY DISAPPEARED
Lighting a candle	The match would light, but both the match flame and candle flame would be small and round and hard to keep lit. Where there is no gravity, density differences do not result in sinking or floating, so there is no convection to deliver needed oxygen to the flame. (Learn about convection in "Where's the Heat?") Oxygen can reach the flame only by diffusion (the drifting of one substance through another as the particles bounce around).
Getting a haircut	If your hair is clean and dry it will most likely stand out in all directions. Scissors will work fine to cut it. The cut pieces will need to be vacuumed up to keep them from littering the air.

Important Note

Maybe you've realized that if gravity really *did* disappear, we wouldn't be writing letters or cutting hair. Earth would leave its orbit around the sun, water would leave its ocean and lake beds, and life would come to an end. Yikes! The good news is that the universe is orderly and the rules of physics never change. Gravity is a side effect of mass, so as long as Earth exists, gravity will keep us and our belongings safely attached to the ground.

15. Where's the Heat?

Vocabulary

Friction: a force against the direction of motion when two surfaces touch; results in heat.

Combustion: burning; combustion is a chemical reaction between oxygen and fuel; for combustion to occur, oxygen, fuel, and heat are needed.

Convection: movement of a gas or liquid caused by temperature difference; warmed fluid becomes less dense and rises.

Law of Conservation of Energy: energy may change forms and locations but, except in nuclear reactions, the total amount of energy that exists does not increase or decrease.

What's Going On?

The normal way to light a match is to strike it on a rough surface. Friction causes heat, and the friction of the match head against the striker causes enough heat to ignite the chemicals in the match head. The heat from the burning match head in turn ignites the wood of the match stick. In this activity, instead of heat from friction, you used the heat from the candle flame to light the match. Before the match touches the flame it gets hot enough to ignite. When you approach *the side* of a flame, the match has to be pretty close—maybe 1/4 inch (0.5 cm) from the flame—to ignite. However, directly *over* the flame it will ignite when it is still about an inch (2.5 cm) away. This tells you that there is more heat above the flame than to the side of it.

Do you know *why* it is hotter above a flame than it is to the side or below? Heat from the flame radiates out equally in *all* directions but the air is constantly floating upward, carrying heat with it. This is caused by density differences in the air. Heat from the flame causes the air to expand. The heated air is less dense than the cooler, surrounding air, so it floats up. (Think of a hot-air balloon and how it rises.) Other air moves in, gets heated, and does the same thing, so much of the flame's heat moves *upward* with the rising air. This up and down circling of the air, or any fluid, around a heat source is called *convection*.

The low end of the candle loses more wax to melting since more of the candle is in the hottest zone over the flame. The wax drips off, reducing the weight of the candle on that side. Like a see-saw, the lighter side moves up, but now the opposite end loses the most wax. This sequence repeats until the candle is gone.

You may have noticed that a candle that would normally burn for hours burns very quickly this way. We usually stand candles up to burn them. The wick constantly carries a little melted wax to the flame where it burns, keeping the flame going. When the candle is held sideways, however, the wax absorbs more heat and melts faster. Most of the wax never burns. It just drips down onto the foil.

The candle flame eventually goes out, but the energy that was released from the candle continues to exist. The flame heated the surrounding air, speeding up the motion of the particles in the air. As the particles moved apart, they spread their energy to other particles. The heat energy gets very spread out by this process but it does not disappear.

Where Else Do You See Convection in Action?

- Using matches. If you have trouble keeping a lighted match burning, look at how you are holding it. If you hold it upright like a candle it will burn slowly and may go out. If you hold it sideways, it will burn faster and be less likely to go out. If you hold the match upside down, it will burn even faster but may burn your fingers, too!
- In stoves, ovens, or outdoor grills, food is placed over the heat source. Natural convection carries the heat up through the food. If you placed food under the fire in an outdoor grill, you would have to wait a long time for your lunch. A broiler in an oven can effectively heat from above because the heated air is trapped and cannot move any higher.
- Home heating. Heaters and heat vents are put close to the floor. The heated air travels up from there.
- Weather systems. Warm air masses will rise up over cold air masses.
- Plate tectonics. Semi-liquid mantle, heated by Earth's core, rises toward the surface, moving plates of Earth's crust in the process.

16. Whirligig Rocketry

Vocabulary

Force: a push or a pull
Center of gravity: the point around which an object spins smoothly
Exhaust nozzle: an opening at the rear of rocket and jet engines where exhaust gases exit

Thrust: the forward force on a rocket from its engines
Trial: one try in an experiment
Average: the sum of a list of values divided by the number of items in the list
Newton's Third Law of Motion: forces come in pairs. For every action force, there is a reaction force that is equal in size and opposite in direction.
Source of error: a flaw in the design of an experiment that can lead to a faulty conclusion.

What's Going On?

The balloon and the air inside push on each other. Sir Isaac Newton recognized that objects always act this way. If you push on a table with your hand, the table pushes back on your hand. You can feel your hand flattening from the table's push. If you punch the wall, the wall punches your hand with the same force but in the opposite direction. It hurts! The balloon and the gas act just this way. The elastic walls of the balloon push the air, moving it out the exhaust nozzle. At the same time, the air pushes the straw and balloon in exactly the opposite direction.

AIR PUSHES STRAW THIS WAY

STRAW PUSHES AIR THIS WAY

The direction the nozzle points is opposite the direction the straw gets pushed. In some nozzle positions the straw spins easily. But if it gets pushed in a direction it can't move because the pin is in the way, little spin results. Does this fit your observations?

As for nozzle size, there is a best nozzle size for a given rocket. With the whirligigs, a smaller nozzle opening increases the total number of spins. A smaller nozzle opening, however, reduces the rate of spin. If the nozzle opening of a rocket is too large, the push on the rocket doesn't last long enough. If it is too small, the rocket doesn't speed up enough. Both the amount of force and the rate of force are important in launching real rockets. Rocket designers use data similar to what you have collected to make sure their engines produce the right amount of force over the right amount of time.

In model rockets and space rockets, the burning of fuel is what produces the pressurized gas to push the rocket upward. Many people think that the rocket needs to push off the launch pad to move, but that is incorrect. The push upward comes from the gases inside the engine. This push on the rocket by the exhaust is called *thrust*.

Another lesson in this activity comes from collecting and analyzing data. While you can get an idea of what's going on by just playing around, to make a strong case for a believable conclusion, experimenters *write down* what they see, and they always do *multiple trials*. The more tries, the more convincing the evidence. They also avoid errors by *keeping all*

conditions, other than the one they are changing on purpose, *constant*. You did this by using the *same* balloon, the *same* technique, and by inflating the balloon to the *same* size. If you had filled the balloon different amounts each time, you would have introduced a *source of error* that would have made some positions appear to be better or worse for spinning than they really are.

17. Pop Can Pedestal

Vocabulary

Strength: the ability to hold up under stress
Compressive strength: the ability to withstand squeezing
Tensile strength: the ability to withstand pulling
Load: the weight a structure carries

What's Going On?

The soft drink can is pretty strong! In the vertical direction it is strong enough to handle the compression of someone standing on it. Its strength is limited, however. When the load is greater than its compressive strength, the can is crushed.

The material of the can, the thickness of the can wall, and the shape of the can are a few of the factors that determine its compressive strength.

The shape of the can is changed when the can is hit by a rubber band. The slight dent caused by the rubber band weakens the wall. The load that was held before is suddenly too great for the weakened can and it collapses.

A tube made from one sheet of paper is pretty strong, too. The type and weight of the paper are factors that determine its exact strength but typical copy paper holds 6 to 7 pounds (about 3 kilograms). A major source of variation is uneven weight distribution on the tube. Doubling the paper does seem to double the strength. Calculate the number of sheets needed to support your weight by the following:

Your weight: _____ ÷ Weight held by one sheet: _____ = Number of sheets: _____

If standing on this number of sheets succeeds, remove one sheet and try again, repeating, if necessary, until the tube is crushed. This will tell you how close your estimate actually was.

18. Ramp

Vocabulary

Engineering: designing objects to serve a purpose; finding solutions to technical problems

Energy: the ability to move something

Potential energy: stored energy

Kinetic energy: active energy; energy of motion

Gravitational potential energy: energy stored by lifting an object; the higher the object, the more gravitational potential energy it has

Friction: resistance to motion when two or more surfaces rub together; produces heat

What's Going On?

You are an engineer! You have designed and built a device to perform a certain job. You used your understanding of physical principles and worked within the limits of your resources. Once you built and examined your structure, you may have found new ways to improve it. Most of the work done by engineers is refining and improving what has come before.

It takes energy to move the Ping-Pong ball. You give the ball gravitational potential energy by lifting it up to the starting point on the ramp. The higher the starting point, the greater the amount of gravitational potential energy. As soon as the ball starts rolling and as long as the ball is moving downward, some of its potential energy is converted into motion (kinetic energy). As the ball rolls, friction from rubbing against the ramp and the air converts some of its kinetic energy into heat. When the ball reaches the bottom of the ramp, its gravitational potential energy is gone. And once the ball comes to a rest, all of its kinetic energy has been changed into heat. The amount of heat is small and quickly spreads out so it is not easily noticed.

Gravitational Potential Energy
   of the elevated ball
     ↓
Kinetic Energy of the rolling ball
     ↓
Heat of the ball, ramp, and air

To get the most rolling time out of the height of the ramp, your ramp needs to be long. To fit above the poster board, the ramp, therefore, must have many turns or switchbacks and many levels of track. With so many levels, the challenge is to design rigid supports that won't let it fall over or sag. Unwrinkled tubes and folded triangular columns work well for supporting posts. The design should also be simple, so it will have few problems and can be built within the time limit. "V"-shaped sections work well for most of the length of the ramp. How they connect to one another all depends on the master plan. Some thought should be given to locating the support structures where they won't get in the way as you build the ramp on and around them.

How to Measure Success

Do you want to know what is considered a good result? That depends on your experience, knowledge, coordination, age, and other factors. Without practice, a time of 5 seconds is above average and 10 seconds is outstanding. With more practice, times up to 30 seconds are possible.

You are the most important judge of how well you do. No matter where you start, improving on a past result means progress. Persistence and willingness to try new ideas are two qualities worth practicing. While you are at it, have fun!

19. Tall Tower

Vocabulary

Base: the bottom of a standing object. It includes any area between supports. For example, the base of a chair is a square that includes all the area within the four legs.

Center of gravity: the point around which the weight of an object is evenly distributed. For an object to stand, its center of gravity must be directly above some part of the base.

What's Going On?

To build a tall tower from one sheet of paper, the tower obviously needs to be slim. There are two common difficulties. One is getting the tower to be strong enough to hold itself up and the other is getting the tower to balance. The designer has to keep both strength and balance in mind. To stand, the center of gravity of the tower must be somewhere directly above the base. If the base is tiny and the tower leans a bit, the center of gravity will not be above the base and the tower will fall. So, it makes sense to make the base bigger in diameter than the rest of the tower. Then you need to work carefully to keep the rest of the tower symmetrical so that the center of gravity stays over the base. Whereas all of the tower's weight is supported by the bottom of the tower, sections higher up only have to support the weight *above* them. So the bottom of the tower needs to be the strongest, the middle can be less strong, and the very top of the tower can be a thin wisp of paper.

How to Measure Success

Do you want to know what is considered a good result? Well, most people can build a tower like this more that 3 feet (91 cm) tall with some time for practice. Only a very few (including professional engineers) succeed in building one over 6 feet tall (183 cm). Realize, though, that what is poor work for one person might be a fine accomplishment for another. It all depends on the person's experience, knowledge, coordination, age, and other factors.

You are the most important judge of how well you do. And, no matter what your first result is, you can demonstrate progress by

improving on it. Being persistent and trying new ideas will help you not only on this project, but it will also help you in most real-life activities.

20. Portable Alarm

Vocabulary

Electron: one of the tiny particles that make up atoms

Electricity: a form of energy; occurs when electrons flow from place to place

Battery: contains stored energy that can be changed into electricity

Chemical reaction: a rearrangement of particles in a substance or substances so that at least one new substance is formed

Energy: the ability to move something

Potential energy: energy in a stored, non-moving form

Chemical potential energy: energy stored in the connections between particles of a substance. Foods, fuels, and batteries are high in this type of energy.

Circuit: the continuous looped path that must exist for electricity to flow from a battery

Short circuit: what occurs when the path of electrical flow skips a device it was supposed to go through. If electrons can directly flow from one battery terminal to another without going through the buzzer, they will do so very quickly, heating the path and using up the battery.

Electrical conductor: a material through which electrons can easily flow; usually metal

Electrical insulator: a material through which electrons cannot flow easily, usually non-metal

What's Going On?

Now that you have built your alarm, you probably understand exactly what works and doesn't work in circuits. If the path is broken, no buzzing. When the path is complete, BUZZ!

The energy to operate the buzzer comes from the battery. Two chemicals are contained separately in the battery, each in contact with one of the battery's two terminals. The chemicals carry out a long-distance chemical reaction through the conductive wires of the circuit. As one gives off electrons, the other snatches up electrons. The electrons flow because one terminal is pushing the electrons and the other is taking them in. The flow of electrons is *electricity*. Without the other chemical, neither can react alone, so if the circuit is opened (path broken), the electricity stops. When the chemicals are almost used up, the battery loses power and eventually quits.

Rechargeable batteries can accept energy to reverse the chemical reaction to start the process all over again. However, non-rechargeable batteries get hot if you try to recharge them and could explode, so be careful.

If you accidentally make a connection between the wrong wires, you may get a *short circuit*. The electricity follows the easiest path. If it can find a route back to the battery without operating any device, *whether that path is actually shorter or not*, it will go that route. As a result, the device will not work, the pathway overheats, and the battery is destroyed. In your alarm, the wires are not insulated. The wire is conductive everywhere, so it is easy to accidentally get a short circuit. Wires in electrical devices that you buy are well insulated to prevent such short circuits. If a short circuit occurs in home wiring, it usually "trips" a circuit breaker or blows a fuse. Fuses and circuit breakers are safety devices that stop the flow of electricity to prevent fires when wiring overheats.

Foods, fuels, and batteries all contain the kind of stored energy called *chemical potential energy*. It's real energy but you can't detect it until you convert it into another form through chemical reactions. Foods, fuels, and batteries are valuable because the chemical reactions they undergo give us power to operate our bodies, cars, planes, power plants, toys, and so much more. Imagine how much money is spent each day on chemical potential energy!

21. Bubble Extravaganza

Vocabulary

Evaporation: a change of state from liquid to gas at the surface of a liquid

Humidity: the amount of water vapor in the air

Cohesion: the attraction of a substance for itself

Convex: curved outward, such as the outer surface of a bubble

Reflection: occurs when light bounces off of a surface

Interference: when two sets of reflected light rays interact to cause additions or subtractions of color

What's Going On?

Durability and Popping

Drying out is a bubble's enemy. Heat, wind, and low humidity are all conditions that speed up evaporation (drying) and so are *not* good conditions for bubble making. If you are outdoors, a humid, windless, overcast day is perfect for bubbles. Just after a rain is nice, too. Glycerin in the solution also helps bubbles last because it slows the evaporation of water. Most dry objects pop bubbles, but wet or soap solution-covered objects don't.

Shape

Almost any object with an opening can be a bubble-making tool. Rubber bands, paper clips, paper cones, and countless other items can be used to make bubbles. Regardless of the shape of the opening, however, single bubbles always end up round like a ball. They may start out sausage shaped from the blowing action, but even these wobble into a sphere, if they last long enough. This has to do with the cohesion of the soap solution. The molecules cling to their neighbors in every direction. These pulls make the bubble elastic like a balloon and cause it to make its surface area small. Of all possible shapes, a sphere has the smallest surface area for its volume.

The Thread Loop

The same elasticity described above causes the thread loop to open to a circle. The soap film pulls the loop in every direction.

Bubble Connections

When two or more bubbles meet, they connect and share an inner wall. The wall between two bubbles of the same size is flat. If one of the bubbles is bigger than the other, the common wall will bulge into the bigger one. When more than two bubbles meet, the common walls always form angles to one another of 120°. This is the same angle found between walls in a honeycomb. Nature is so orderly!

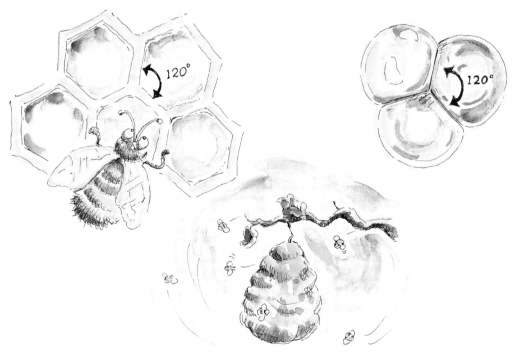

Bubble Colors

The shiny surface of bubbles is good for reflecting light from the surroundings. Like the view in a convex mirror, you can see a distorted reflection of the room or your own face in a bubble. (Where did you get such a big nose, by the way?) Whereas some of the reflected light bounces off the outside of the bubble wall, the rest of it bounces off the inside of the bubble wall and this tiny difference causes a big difference in the light's color.

The reflected light rays from the two surfaces interact or interfere with one another, resulting in interesting colors. This interference is the same phenomenon that causes the shimmery colors of pearls, bird feathers, and gasoline on water. As a bubble begins to lose water to drying, the thickness of the bubble wall changes. This changes the light ray interactions, and new colors appear. When the bubble wall gets very thin, just before popping, it turns colorless. You can predict just when a bubble will pop by watching for this color change.

22. Delicious Ice Cream . . . Yum!

Vocabulary

Change of state: transformation of a substance from one state of matter (solid, liquid, or gas) to another

Freezing: a change of state from liquid to solid

Freezing point: the temperature at which freezing of a substance occurs

Freezing point depression: the lowering of a freezing point caused by the presence of dissolved substances

Heat conductor: material that moves heat easily from one location to another. Metals are good conductors.

Heat insulator: material that does not move heat well from one place to another. Wood and plastic are insulators.

What's Going On?

Making ice cream involves changing the state of the cream mixture from a liquid to a solid. There are three states of matter we see on Earth: solid, liquid, and gas. A gas that loses enough heat turns into a liquid. A liquid that loses enough heat freezes into a solid.

Your cream mixture freezes at about 14° F (−10° C). Ice, water, and salt surround your ice cream can. Ice water alone can never be colder than 32° F (0° C), so it is not cold enough to freeze the cream. Adding the salt to ice, however, does three things:

1. It lowers the freezing point of the water to approximately 1° F (−17° C).
2. It melts some of the ice in the bucket.
3. It lowers the temperature of the salt/ice/water mixture.

Why does it do all this? Ice exists because, at low temperatures, water particles are attracted to one another and hold each other in place. The salt lowers the water's freezing point when it dissolves because it gets in the way of the attraction between water particles. The ice melts as a result of this interference. With salt particles in the way, the water particles must get even colder before they can lock into position as solid ice. Since melting requires energy, heat gets stolen from the ice water, making it colder than it was without the salt. If the ice bath gets down to 10° F (−12° C), the cream chills down past its own freezing point of about 14° F (−10° C), turning into solid ice cream.

The texture and quality of the ice cream is determined, in part, by the size of the ice crystals that form as it freezes. The scraping

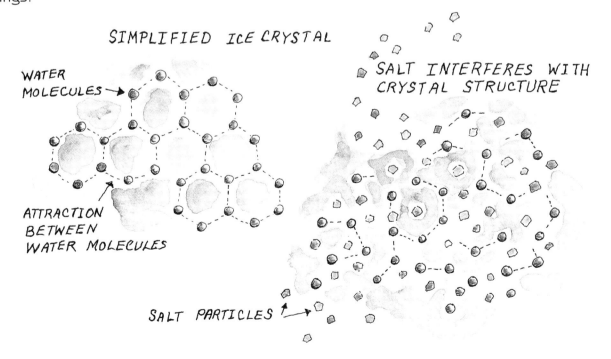

SIMPLIFIED ICE CRYSTAL

WATER MOLECULES →

ATTRACTION BETWEEN WATER MOLECULES

SALT INTERFERES WITH CRYSTAL STRUCTURE

SALT PARTICLES →

and stirring you do prevents the crystals from getting too large and keeps the ice cream smooth, not grainy. The stirring also helps trap tiny air bubbles that lighten the texture of the ice cream.

Successful freezing depends on choosing the right materials to direct heat away from the cream. Heat moves from warmer areas to cooler areas. Since metal is a good heat conductor, it's a good material for holding the cream. The metal can conducts heat away from the cream into the colder ice. The cream cools as a result. A spoon made of metal would be a bad choice, however, because it would conduct heat from the warm air and your warm hand into the cream. Plastic or wood make better spoons for this since they are insulators.

CREAM WARMS

THAT'S NOT GOOD!

CREAM COOLS — THAT'S GOOD!

Where Else Do You See Conduction and Insulation?

In a hot car, metals may burn you as they effectively conduct their heat to your cooler skin. Fabrics in the same car will be just as warm but are poor at conducting their heat and so do not feel so hot.

Coats and blankets you use to keep warm don't *provide* heat, they just keep the heat of your body from being conducted away. They are insulators.

Air and other gases are insulators. Window manufacturers make use of this fact when they make double-pane windows with gas in between the glass layers.

Your home probably has insulation to conserve heat and/or air conditioning. In the winter in areas where snow piles up on rooftops, you can sometimes tell which houses are poorly insulated. On these houses, the rooftop snow melts as heat from the house rises up through the roof, wasting money and energy. Many gas and electric companies will do free home audits to show you where you can save energy by improving insulation.

23. Meringue Dessert Cups

Vocabulary

Polymer: a large molecule made of a long chain of smaller units

Protein: one category of polymers found in living things. Hair, nails, and muscle are high in protein. Egg whites are about 10% protein.

Denatured protein: a protein molecule that has had its natural, three-dimensional shape changed

Chemistry: the science of substances and how changes in substances occur

What's Going On?

Egg white is about 90% water and 10% protein. The protein molecules, though very large as molecules go, start out as compact blobs that are small enough to dissolve in the water of the egg white. Vigorously whipping the egg white changes the structure of the protein molecules into a new three-dimensional shape that is looser and more spread out. Tiny air bubbles are also formed by the whipping action and trapped. The change in the shape of the protein molecules changes their solubility. Now the protein will not dissolve in the water. Instead, it forms a semi-solid net that gives the meringue its shape and holds the well-dispersed water and air bubbles in place. The change in the structure of the protein molecule is called *denaturing*. The sugar that is added dissolves into the water.

The oven-drying step removes most of the water so that the meringue cups become crisp and hold their shape. Once dry, the meringue will gradually reabsorb moisture from the air. If the dessert cups are not kept in an air-tight container, they will get soft and crumbly from this absorbed water. Leaving out the cream of tartar reduces the fluffiness of the meringue.

Cream of tartar is an acid. It helps denature the protein molecules to make the foam and then it stabilizes the walls of the air bubbles in the foam so they last. Putting yolk in the meringue results in wimpy, low-volume foam. Powdered sugar, however, works well for this kind of meringue. The smaller-sized sugar crystals dissolve faster in the egg white mixture and make a nice, light foam.

The science of substances and their changes is called *chemistry*. You've surely heard that word before! The average person who cooks might be called a *food technician*. They follow recipes, but don't really know why they do each step. Great chefs, however, are often food *chemists*. They understand the effect of each ingredient and the consequences of heating and stirring on the structure of the molecules. They know how each step translates into the flavor and texture of the food and therefore are skilled at controlling them. There are many jobs and careers in food science besides cooks and chefs. Did you know you could be a meat engineer? A flavor chemist? A package designer?

24. Fabulous Play Gloop

Vocabulary

Fluid: a liquid or a gas; able to flow
Polymer: a long skinny molecule made of smaller units linked together in a chain
Viscosity: resistance to flow; the more viscous a fluid, the slower it flows
Adhesion: sticking to another object
Cohesion: sticking to itself

What's Going On?

White glue contains long molecules called *polymers*. Polymers are constructed of a chain of repeating units like a string of beads. One of the ingredients in the liquid starch is Borax, which, when it meets the polymer molecules in the glue, links them together at many points. The new cross-linked polymers have less freedom to flow.

POLYMER MOLECULE

CROSS LINKED POLYMER MOLECULE

This is what turns the runny glue and liquid starch into the more viscous, semisolid Gloop. The linking also makes the glue more cohesive than adhesive. For the glue to hold together when you work with it, its attraction to itself (its cohesion) must be stronger than its adhesion to your skin.

BEHAVE YOURSELF!

GLOOP!

Gloop is called a "non-Newtonian fluid." This just means that it is a fluid that doesn't behave quite like other fluids. Factors other than temperature affect its viscosity. You probably noticed that the Gloop gets more firm while you are handling it but when you let it relax, it flows. When stretched quickly, it snaps off like a solid, but when stretched gently, there seems to be no limit to its elasticity.

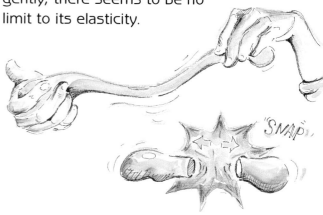

SNAP

A list of physical properties of Gloop could include:

pale blue
shiny
squishy
doesn't bounce
feels wet
tears when pulled hard; stretches when
    pulled slowly
can form thin, transparent sheets
will form bubbles
sinks in water
when set down it slowly loses shape,
    getting flatter and flatter
sticks to paper and fabric
doesn't stick to solid surfaces like glass
    or countertop
brittle when frozen

25. T-shirt Designs

(See the explanation for Radiant Color on page 134 for more information)

Vocabulary

Solvent: a substance that dissolves other substances

Capillary action: the movement of a liquid through tiny openings in a solid

Permanent ink: ink that does not dissolve in water

What's Going On?

Doing the "Radiant Color" process on fabric requires different pens and a different solvent. You use permanent ink so the color won't disappear when you wash the shirt. You use rubbing alcohol because it will dissolve the ink and move it along the fabric. Water won't move the permanent ink at all. Heat from an iron helps bond the color to the fabric when you are finished.

As in "Radiant Color," the alcohol solvent moved along the fabric by capillary action. The ink moved along with the alcohol, but you probably got more color smearing than separation into different pigments. Cotton fabric and rubbing alcohol just aren't the best combination for getting distinct bands of color. The permanent pen pigments dissolve but have such similar attractions for the alcohol and fabric that they don't separate well. The moving alcohol just smears them. A different solvent could be chosen to better separate the pigments, but most solvents are more dangerous to use than rubbing alcohol. Anyway, the spreading effect looks cool.

INDEXES AND APPENDIX

Physical Science Concept Index

National Science Education Standards Matrix

NATIONAL SCIENCE EDUCATION STANDARDS
OF THE NATIONAL RESEARCH COUNCIL, 1996, GRADES 5–8

SCIENCE AS INQUIRY STANDARD (QUOTED)

Abilities Necessary to Do Scientific Inquiry

Identify questions that can be answered through scientific investigation

Design and conduct a scientific investigation

Use appropriate tools and techniques to gather, analyze, and interpret data

Develop descriptions, explanations, predictions, and models using evidence

Think critically and logically to make the relationships between evidence and explanations

Recognize and analyze alternative explanations and predictions

Communicate scientific procedures and explanations

Use mathematics in all aspects of scientific inquiry

PHYSICAL SCIENCE CONTENT STANDARD (ABBREVIATED)

Properties and Changes of Properties of Matter

A substance has characteristic properties, such as density, independent of sample size

Chemical reactions form new substances while conserving mass

There are more than 100 elements that combine to produce compounds

Motion and Forces

The motion of an object can be quantified by position, direction, motion, and speed

An object not subjected to a net force will continue to move straight at a constant speed

Unbalanced forces will cause changes in the speed or direction of an object's motion

Transfer of Energy

Energy takes many forms and can be converted from form to form

Heat moves predictably from warmer objects to cooler ones

Light interacts with matter by transmission, absorption, or scattering

Circuits transfer electrical energy from heat, light, sound, and chemical changes

Energy is transferred into or out of a system in most chemical and nuclear reactions

The sun is a major source of energy for changes on the earth's surface

	1	2	3	4	5	6	7	8	9	10	11	12	13	14	15	16	17	18	19	20	21	22	23	24	25
ACTIVITIES																									
	X	X	X	X		X	X	X	X		X	X	X		X	X	X				X		X	X	
	X	X	X	X	X	X	X	X	X	X	X	X	X		X	X	X				X		X	X	
	X	X	X	X	X	X	X	X	X	X	X	X	X	X	X	X	X				X		X	X	
	X	X	X	X	X	X	X	X	X	X	X	X	X	X	X	X	X	X	X	X	X	X	X	X	X
	X	X	X	X	X	X	X	X	X	X	X	X	X	X	X	X	X	X	X	X	X	X	X	X	X
														X											
		X	X	X			X	X	X		X	X	X		X	X	X		X	X		X		X	X
		X		X							X					X	X								
	X			X	X	X	X	X			X				X						X	X	X	X	X
	X	X		X																			X	X	
																								X	
		X									X		X		X	X									
							X	X	X			X	X	X	X	X	X								
		X	X				X	X	X	X	X	X	X	X	X	X	X						X		X
		X	X									X	X		X	X					X		X		
			X												X								X		
																					X				
																					X				

Graphing Appendix

Graphs are information pictures. To people with a little experience, they make data understandable at a glance.

Two types of graphs, **bar graphs** and **line graphs**, are used to show experiment results. A third type, a **circle graph**, is used when you want to show the relationship of parts to a whole.

In an experiment, you try to find the effect of one variable, called the *manipulated variable,* on another variable, called the *responding variable*. In "Explosion," for example, you might test the effect of **type of liquid** (manipulated variable) on **the time it takes the vial to explode** (responding variable).

To be able to create a bar or line graph, your responding variable must be a measurement or a count so that you can put the results on a number line. This variable goes on the vertical (y) axis so that the reader's eye moves UP when values are large and DOWN when values are small.

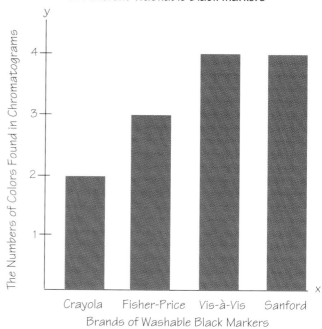

The Numbers of Colors Found in Chromatograms of Different Washable Black Markers

Bar Graph

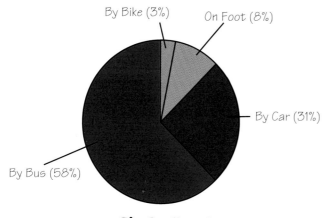

How Anderson High School Students Get to School

Circle Graph

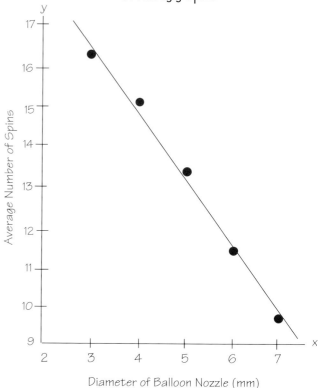

The Effect of Nozzle Diameter on the Number of Whirligig Spins

Line Graph

If the data from the other variable cannot be put on a number line (for example, they are brand names or colors or types of vegetables), then you make a bar graph.

How to Make a Bar Graph

Example: Making a Bar Graph
Let's say your data table from an "Explosion" experiment was as follows:

TIME TO EXPLODE (SEC)			
	TYPE OF LIQUID		
	WATER	MILK	COLA
Trial #1	2.6	3.0	1.7
Trial #2	2.8	2.6	1.9
Trial #3	1.8	3.3	2.0
Average	2.4	3.0	1.9

This data should be made into a bar graph. The responding variable, *time to explode* can be put on a number line while the other variable, *type of liquid*, cannot.

1. Get a sheet of graph paper* and a well-sharpened pencil. Your graph will be made to fill the sheet. Choose which way to place the page.

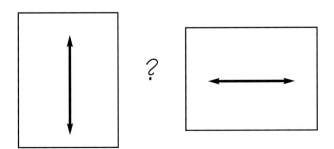

*Graph paper is provided at the end of this book.

2. Use a ruler to draw in the vertical (*y*) and horizontal (*x*) axes. You need to leave enough space outside the lines for labels, so indent them several squares from the edges of the paper. Also end the lines several squares before you reach the edge of the paper.

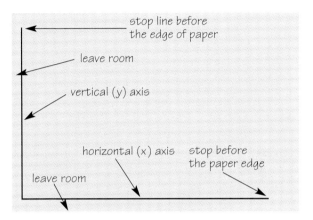

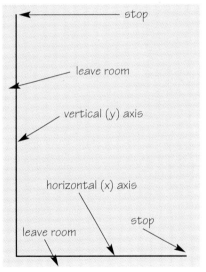

3. On the horizontal (*x*) axis, you are going to mark off equal-width bars with spaces in between them. Properly dividing up any graph axis is the hardest job in graphing. Sometimes, you can see instantly how to do it or you can work it out with trial and error. To figure out how many graph paper boxes to use per bar and space, follow these steps while you think about their logic:

a. Count the number of graph paper boxes available on the axis.

b. Divide the number of boxes (use a calculator if you like) by the number of bars you have, and round your answer *down* to the nearest whole number.

c. Split that number into two parts, one for the space before the bar, and one for the bar itself. In other words, for the answer 9, you might decide to make each space 3 boxes wide and each bar 6 boxes wide, or 4 boxes for spaces and 5 boxes for bars.

d. Mark off the bars and spaces on the horizontal axis. Write in labels centered below the bars in any reasonable order. You might want to order them from tallest to shortest— or shortest to tallest.

4. Now you will create the number line on the vertical (*y*) axis so that your highest value will land toward the top of the paper. Realize that your data values are NOT the values you put along the axis unless it just happens to work out that way. You will label the axis next to the graph paper *lines*, not the *spaces*. You might see instantly how to spread out the number line or you can work it out with trial and error. Or, you can follow these steps:

a. Pick an even number just above the highest value of the data to be the end of the number line for the axis.

b. Divide this number by the number of boxes you can use on the graph paper (count them).

c. Round your answer *up* to a nice, round value such as 0.1, 0.2, 0.5, 1, 2, 5,

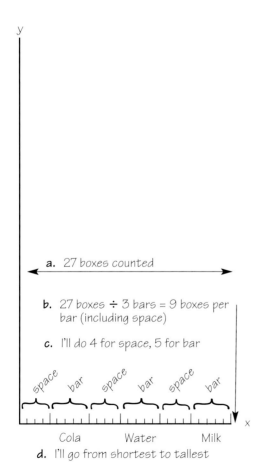

a. 27 boxes counted

b. 27 boxes ÷ 3 bars = 9 boxes per bar (including space)

c. I'll do 4 for space, 5 for bar

space bar space bar space bar

Cola   Water   Milk

d. I'll go from shortest to tallest

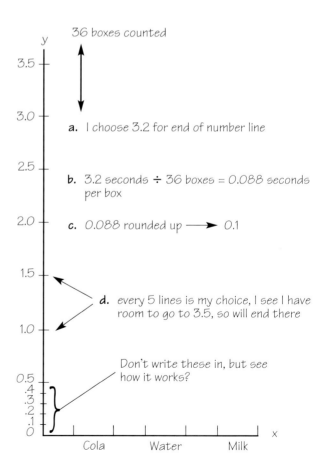

36 boxes counted

a. I choose 3.2 for end of number line

b. 3.2 seconds ÷ 36 boxes = 0.088 seconds per box

c. 0.088 rounded up ⟶ 0.1

d. every 5 lines is my choice, I see I have room to go to 3.5, so will end there

Don't write these in, but see how it works?

Cola   Water   Milk

10, 20, 50, 100 etc. This will be the value of each box on the graph paper.

d. Write in the number value for every two, five, or ten lines.

5. Add labels outside each axis. Unless the vertical scale is a count, units (such as *meters* or *seconds*) go in parentheses next to the label.

6. Use the ruler to help you estimate the appropriate height of the bars, draw them, and shade them in.

7. Add a descriptive title at the top. Hey, that is looking good!

A line graph is done when data from BOTH variables can be put on number lines.

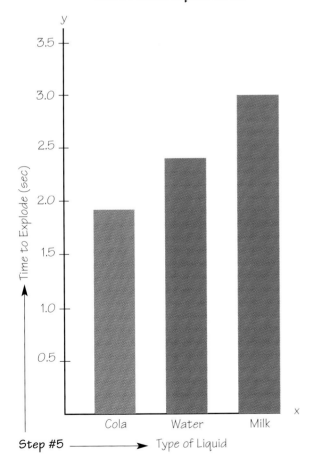

The Average Time for Film Cans to Explode with Different Liquids Inside

Step #5 ⟶ Type of Liquid

How to Make a Line Graph

Example: Making a Line Graph

Let's say your data table from "Explosion" looked like this:

	TIME TO EXPLODE (SEC)			
Water Temperatures:	**35°F**	**50°F**	**65°F**	**80°F**
Trial #1	35.2	13.3	5.7	2.6
Trial #2	41.6	15.6	6.0	2.9
Trial #3	37.0	14.5	7.2	2.2
Average	37.9	14.5	6.3	2.6

This data should be made into a line graph because both variables, the *water temperature* and the *time to explode* can be put onto number lines. The time was the outcome, the responding variable, and so it will go on the vertical (*y*) axis.

1. Get a sheet of graph paper and a well-sharpened pencil. Your graph will be made to fill the sheet. Choose which way to place the page.

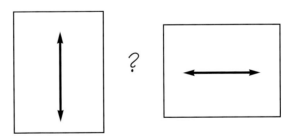

2. Use a ruler to draw in the vertical (*y*) and horizontal (*x*) axes. You must leave enough space outside the lines for labels, so indent them several squares from the edges of the paper. Also end the lines a few squares before reaching the edge of the page.

3. As with bar graphs, the responding variable (your outcome), goes on the vertical (*y*) axis. The other variable is called the manipulated variable and it goes . . . you guessed it, on the horizontal (*x*) axis! The manipulated variable either changes naturally, such as the time or the month, *or* it is set by the experimenter, such as water temperature.

4. Number each axis in even intervals so that the smallest value lands fairly close to the origin (where the axes meet) and the largest value lands near the opposite end of the paper. This step is the hardest part of making the graph. You might see instantly how to do it or you might work it out with trial and error. The following directions work well especially if you think as you go:

For one axis at a time,

a. Pick round numbers just below the lowest data value and just above the

highest to be the beginning and end of the number line for the axis.

b. Subtract the lower value that you selected from the higher one.

c. Divide your answer by the number of boxes you can use on the graph paper (count them).

d. Round your answer *up* to a nice, round value such as 0.1, 0.2, 0.5, 1, 2, 5, 10, 20, 50, 100, etc. This will be the value of each box on the graph paper.

e. Write in the value of every two, five, or ten lines.

5. Add the variable labels and units outside each axis.

For Vertical (y) Axis:

a. My first thought is to go from 0 to 40. But looking ahead I see there are 36 boxes available. If I use 2 to 38, then I will get 1 per box, which is better!

b. 38 − 2 = 36

c. 36 seconds ÷ 36 boxes = 1 second per box

d. no rounding needed. Lucky! (and smart)

e. I'll label every 5 lines

For Horizontal (x) Axis:

a. below: 30   above: use 80 itself

b. 80 − 30 = 50

c. 50 ÷ 26 boxes = 1.92

d. 1.92 rounds up to 2

e. I'll label every 5 boxes

Values on an axis do not need to start at 0.

The Effect of Water Temperature on the Time it Takes Film Cans to Explode

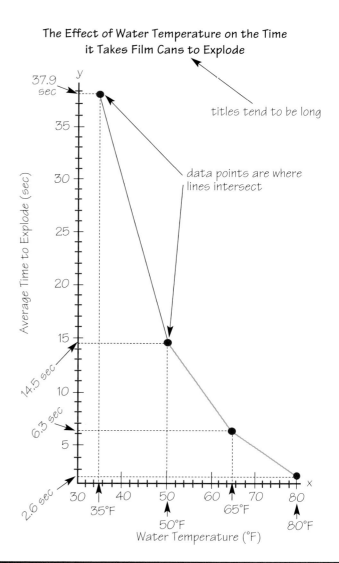

titles tend to be long

data points are where lines intersect

6. Plot the points. For each point this requires estimating where the data values fall on the number line of each axis and then following imaginary lines to the right from the vertical axis and up from the horizontal axis until they intersect.
7. When all points are plotted, connect the points with a pencil line.*
8. Add a descriptive title to the top of the page, and you are done!

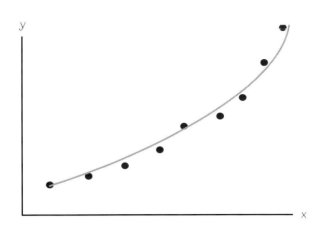

*Best Fit Curve

When you have quite a few data points, it is better to draw what is called a "best fit curve" than connect the points. What you do is stand back and look at the trend your graph shows. Then draw the line to be smooth and continuous. (It may be curved or straight.) It's OK to miss some or even all of the points as long as you follow the trend they seem to show. If the line misses some points, you should miss about as many above the line as below the line. The best fit curve assumes there was some experimental error. It is your estimate of the true results of your study.

The line graph at the beginning of this appendix was drawn with a best fit curve.

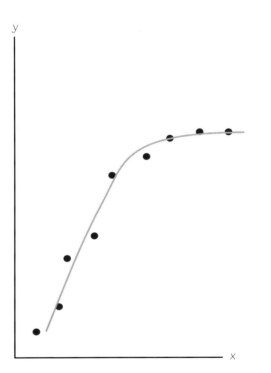

Examples of Best Fit Curves

Key to Metric Abbreviations

Units of Length

mm = millimeter (or .001 meter)

cm = centimeter (or .01 meter)

m = meter

Units of Mass

g = gram

kg = kilogram (or 1,000 grams)

Units of Volume

mL = milliliter (or .001 liter)

L = liter

Units of Temperature

°C = degrees Celsius

PINE HILL MIDDLE SCHOOL
LIBRARY